Operating Systems

A New Perspective

Operating Systems

A New Perspective

Vakkalanka Krishna Chaitanya

CBS

CBS PUBLISHERS & DISTRIBUTORS

NEW DELHI • BANGALORE (INDIA)

ISBN : 81-239-1012-6

First Edition: 2003

Production Director : Vinod K. Jain

Published by :
Satish Kumar Jain for CBS Publishers & Distributors,
4596/1-A, 11 Darya Ganj, New Delhi - 110 002 (India)
E-mail : cbspubs@dcl3.vsnl.net.in
Website : http://www.cbspd.com

Branch Office :
Seema House, 2975, 17th Cross, K.R. Road,
Bansankari 2nd Stage, Bangalore - 560070
Fax : 080-6771680 • E-mail : cbsbng@vsnl.net

Printed at :
Asia Printograph, Shahdara, Delhi - 110 032

Dedicated to my parents

Preface

This is my sincere attempt to provide the student community with a helpful material on Operating Systems. A good amount of effort has been put in this project to make all the 15 chapters concise and informative. The material is supported with a rich graphics set to make the topics easier to understand.

I believe that the students would find it helpful to learn theory being assisted with practical analogies that are used through out the book wherever a particular topic appears complex.

At the end of each chapter appear review questions that aim at testing how well the reader assimilated the theory.

A proper knowledge of what's happening '*inside*' is essential for any programmer who aims at designing a functionally perfect and architecturally complex system. This book helps serious systems programmers understand the ground theory fast to jump to the programming part.

This material could also be used as a readymade compendium to refer to the basics all the time with less effort.

This book is the outcome of a painstaking effort of more than 2 years. I will be very much grateful to everybody who helped me all the way. This idea would not have been realized had I not received timely moral help from many of my mentors. I would like to make use of this opportunity to thank them all. In particular, I would like to extend my sincere thanks to Sri B. Ravindranath, former HOD, CSE, VRS engineering college; Sri K. Ramachandra, HOD, English, VRS engineering college;

Smt. Padmaja madam, lecturer, ECE, VRS engineering college; Sri P. Srinivasa Rao, lecturer, ME, VRS engineering college; Sri Govind Swaminathan, M/S SCITECH Publications, Chennai.

I shall mention with a sincere grateful feeling the continuous help rendered by my dearest friend Mr. Ramesh Vedantam right from the day I shared with him my idea of writing this book. I can't imagine accomplishing this project without his moral and technical help.

I thank all my juniors who have reviewed with interest the material and pointed out the mistakes.

I will be grateful to Mr. Ambuj Kumar Niranjan, my companion in many enterprises, for his guidance in the last minute and I sincerely appreciate the valuable directions of Mr. Sivakamesh Thota about completing the awesome job of drawing the figures with much ease.

And, here are my special acknowledgements to Mr. Kesava Reddy Talupuru for standing through out as the silent destination for the ever encrypted streams of my feelings. I have been a great fan of the strength of his patience and the serenity of his vigorous hard work.

This 'thank you' note would be incomplete if I fail to mention the name of my partner, guide, mentor and philosopher Mr. Sriramulu Appana. He is the person who acquainted me with the term Logic.

Finally, I would like to say a regardful thanks to my brother Sri Prasad KBH Vakkalanka, for his help in developing the content of the book and in designing the figures. I shall thank affectionately Ms. Madhuri Vakkalanka, my little sister for constantly looking forward with hope and zeal to seeing the book brought out.

A lot of effort has been put in this project to bring out an error-free book. However, I am candid in admitting the fact that there could have crept in some errors. I request the reader to bring any such mistakes to my notice, if found. I would be open to constructive comments and logical criticism about any part of this book.

Thank you and good luck.

Vakkalanka Krishna Chaitanya
Salt Lake City
11th April, 2003.

Contents

CHAPTER 1

History and Evolution

Introduction

Before exploring the ocean of Operating Systems, it is worth having a glance over their history and evolution. This introductory chapter, which starts with the basic definition of computer, explains the factors that necessitated the development of operating systems.

1.1 What is a Computer?

A computer is an electronic device that processes the input given to it and produces the result in the required format. Any data required to perform a particular calculation forms the *input*. The user feeds this input to the computer using input devices like keyboard, mouse etc. The computer then processes this data and produces the *output*. According to the requirements of the user, this output is then directed to the output devices like monitor, printer etc.

A typical computer system consists of three major components: CPU, Memory and I/O devices.

- *CPU:* It is the other name for processor (in a uniprocessor system). CPU stands for **C**entral

Processing **U**nit. It is the heart of any computer. It controls the operation of the computer and performs all the data processing functions.

- *Memory:* It is the place that stores the programs and the data required for the operations. This memory is of two types: main memory and secondary memory. Main memory is volatile in nature unlike secondary memory.
- *I/O devices:* These are very useful in conveying the input to the computer and the output to the user. They act as the mediators between the computer and the user for data exchange.

1.2 Operating Systems & Computer Systems

The current availability of the highly sophisticated operating systems, whose efficiency is bound only by the imagination of the user, has a very close relationship with the development of computer systems in the past three centuries.

In fact, operating systems are developed to enhance the ease in using the hardware. Later, some changes were made in the design of the hardware to simplify the operating systems. This process repeated as a cycle until the presently available versatile operating systems are developed.

1.2.1 History

The computer, three centuries back, was not electronic in nature. Instead, it was a huge mechanical device consisting of gears, wheels, cogs etc. into which the user had to go to operate it. Even in the next generation systems, the huge size posed several problems. Although the gears, wheels etc. were absent in these computers the employment of vacuum tubes made these electronic computers very huge.

The invention of transistor in 1947 literally brought a revolution in the development of electronic devices. It reduced the cost and size of the computer and also improved the reliability of the system. Later, the assembly and high-level languages simplified the job of the programmer to a good extent.

However, the operation of the system became more complex because of the I/O devices being used those days. There used to be many steps in executing a small program.

For example, if the user wants to execute a FORTRAN program, the sequence of operations would be: loading the FORTRAN compiler tape, running the compiler, unloading the compiler tape, loading the assembler tape, running the assembler, unloading the assembler tape, loading the object program and then finally, running the object program. Any error, if occurred, would necessitate the user to start again with the first step.

As is evident, all these steps would consume a lot of time during most of which the CPU sits idle. But in those days, because of the cost, maximum utilization of the CPU was the main criterion.

Hence, the concept of *batching* was introduced. In this technique, **jobs with similar needs are batched together and executed as a group**.

For example, suppose that an operator has received 5 jobs: two in COBOL and three in FORTRAN, the order being FORTRAN, COBOL, FORTRAN, COBOL, and FORTRAN. If the operator executed them in the same order, he would have to setup for FORTRAN, then for COBOL, then again for FORTRAN and so on.

To avoid this difficulty, the three FORTRAN jobs are run together as a batch and the two COBOL programs are run as another batch. In this way, a lot of operating time could be saved. Prior to these batch systems, the user, operator, system analyst, designer etc. were all one and the same.

The introduction of batch systems contributed to the improved CPU utilization by making each person different from one another. In batch systems, the task of the programmer was just to write the programs and leave them to the operator. The operator would then divide them into separate batches and later would run each batch separately.

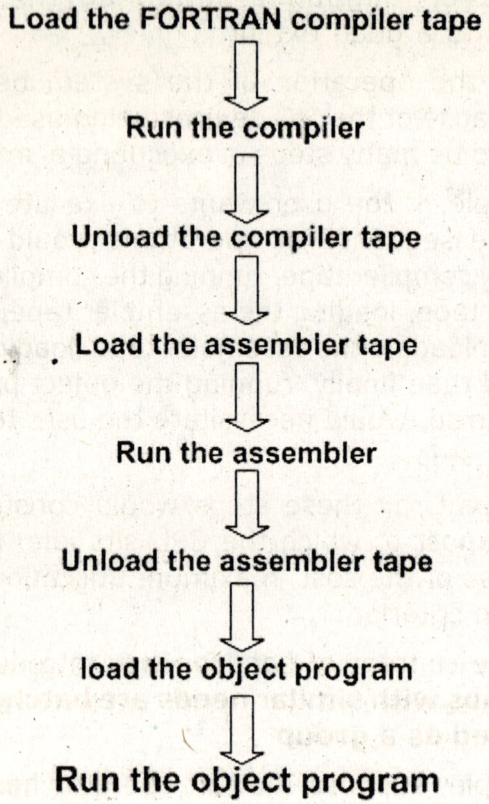

Figure 1.1 *Illustration of the typical steps in program execution*

1.2.2 The origin

However, simply batching the jobs could not yield good results because the transition from one job to another was still being made manually and as a result the CPU was sitting idle again.

Then what could be the remedy? The solution is to **eliminate the human involvement in job sequencing** i.e., to make the sequencing of jobs *automatic*. When one job is run successfully, the control should automatically be transferred to another job. This idea was the main drive behind the development of the first inchoate operating system.

The very first operating system was a simple program

known as *resident monitor*. It was so named because it always resides in the memory. As is required, the resident monitor is invoked automatically immediately after the system is switched on. With the help of control cards all the information about the programs to be executed and their required data etc. were directly provided to the resident monitor.

Each job has a specific number of control cards. The resident monitor loads a particular program into memory when a control card asks it to do so. Then the control is transferred to that program.

After executing completely, that program returns the control to the resident monitor. And then, the resident monitor reads the next control card, loads the next program and transfers the control to that program and this cycle is repeated until all the control cards are interpreted for a particular job. Then, the monitor starts with the next job.

In this way, the batch operating systems functioned well. As is obvious, there is no interaction between the user and the job while the job is being executed. The user prepares the job and submits it. And, the output is produced when the job is completed. Depending upon the number of computations, delays and many other factors, a particular job may take several seconds, minutes, hours or even days.

Thus, even the automatic job sequencing also could not keep the CPU continuously busy. The input devices, card readers for example, were mechanical in nature. The speed of their operation was much less than that of the electronic processor. Hence, the processor must sit idle for a long time during the period a process executes.

1.3 Offline Processing and Spooling

A significant progress was observed when magnetic tapes were introduced as the mediators between card readers and CPU.

Prior to this, as it has been observed, the card reader used to read the data from the cards and convey it to the CPU, which would then process that data and direct the output to the line printer. It is known as *on-line* processing. Because the speed of a typical card reader is very much less than that of the CPU the CPU sits idle for a major amount of time.

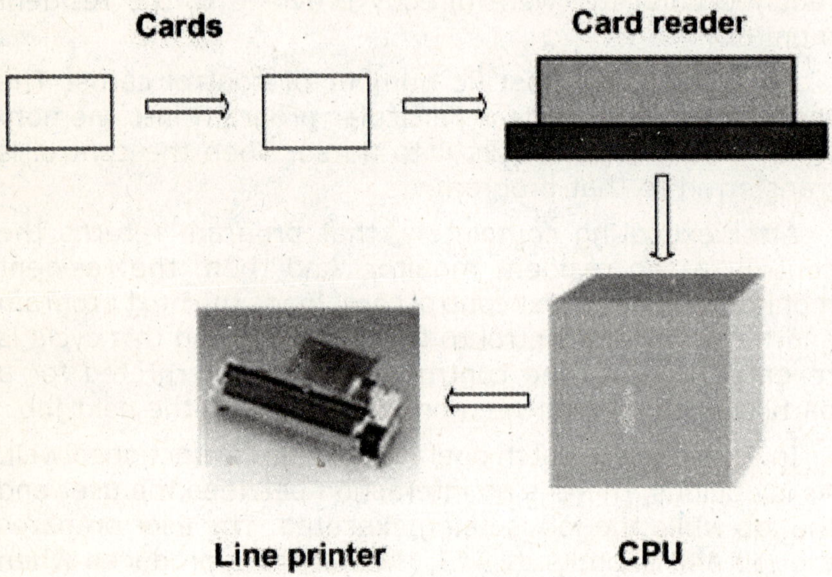

Figure 1.2 *Online processing*

As a remedy to this, the help of magnetic tapes was taken. First, before turning the system on, the magnetic tape is completely filled with the data of the cards. Then the tape is taken to the CPU manually, mounted on the tape drive and then the CPU is turned on.

Now, the CPU reads the data from this magnetic tape instead of reading from the cards directly. Similarly, the output from the CPU is written on to another tape and then that tape is taken to the line printer to print the contents. That means, the card reader and the line printer are operated off-line. Hence, this method is known as *off-line* processing.

The advantage of this method was that the CPU was not constrained by the speed of the card readers. However, the magnetic tapes, being *sequential-access* devices, could not serve the purpose completely. Hence, in most systems,

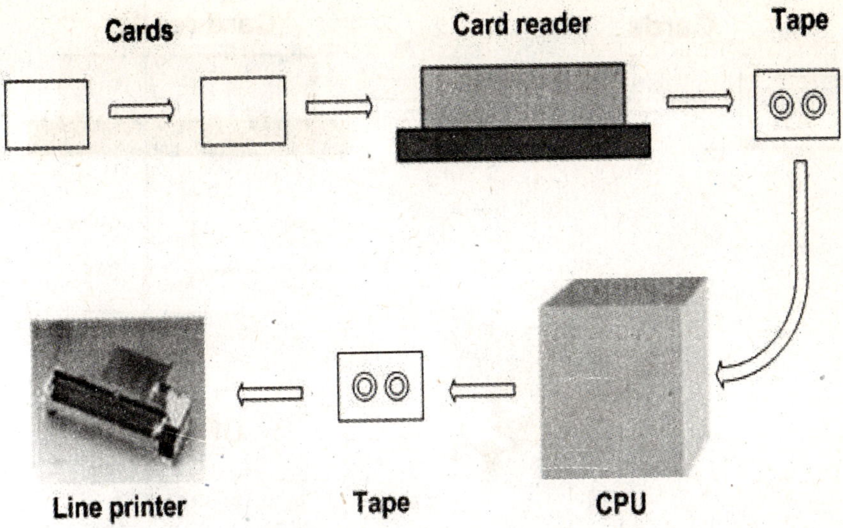

Figure 1.3 *Off-line processing*

these magnetic tapes were replaced by magnetic disks, which are random access devices. Since disks allow random jumping, the CPU could access data of a particular job from a specific area and meanwhile, the output of another job could be directed to the line printer. That means the computation of one job may be overlapped with the I/O of another job. This concept is known as Spooling, which is the acronym for **S**imultaneous **P**eripheral **O**perations **O**n-**L**ine.

In spooling, the cards are read to the disk directly. The operating system keeps a table consisting of the details of the locations of card images.

In a broad view, spooling uses the magnetic disk as a very large buffer to read as many input files and to write as many output files as possible. Spooling can also be used to process data at remote sites with the help of certain communication paths.

In this way, spooling is extremely useful. It could keep both the CPU and I/O devices working at much higher rates.

1.4 Multiprogramming

As a result of spooling, several jobs are stored on a direct-

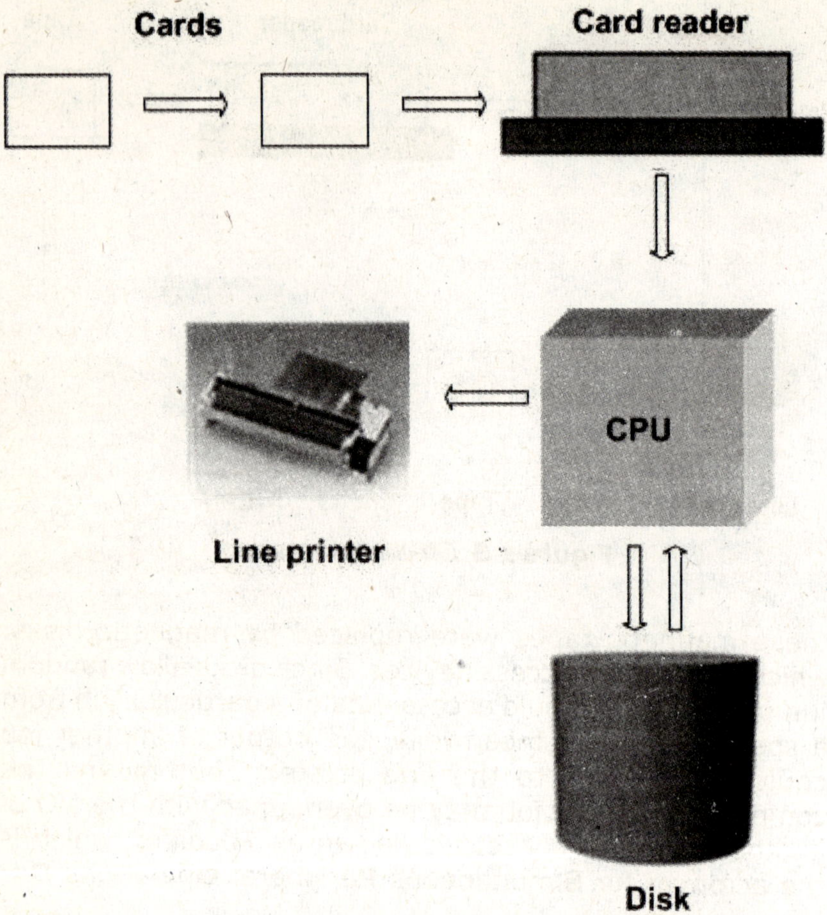

Figure 1.4 *Spooling*

access device, say, a magnetic disc. The availability of more than one job at the same time to the CPU brings into light 'job scheduling'. The most powerful aspect of job scheduling is the ability to *multiprogram*. Multiprogramming schedules the jobs in such a way that the CPU has always a job to work with. Thus, the utilization of CPU increases very much.

Before explaining this concept, it is worth mentioning an important point here. In the secondary or permanent memory there will be several jobs. For any job to be executed it should be brought into the active memory.

That means, before the CPU starts executing any job, the operating system brings it into the main memory. If the main memory can accommodate more than one job, all those jobs are brought into the memory by the operating system.

Now the concept of multiprogramming is as explained - The operating system picks up one of the available jobs and begins to execute it. Eventually, the job may need to wait for a particular task to be performed. This task may be mounting a tape or typing a command etc.

In multiprogrammed systems, then, unlike in nonmulti-programmed systems the CPU would not sit idle. It switches to another job and begins to execute it. If the new job also needs to wait, the CPU again switches to another job and so on. Eventually, the first job finishes waiting and gets the CPU back. In this way, the CPU has always something to execute and hence it will never sit idle.

Figure 1.5 gives an idea about how different jobs are kept in the main memory.

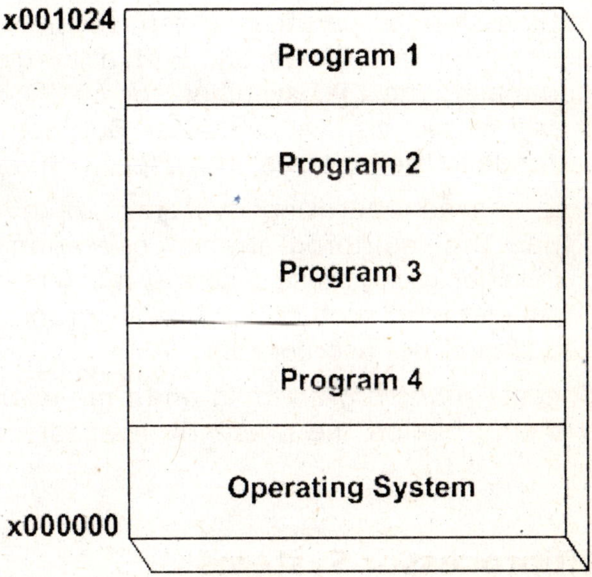

Figure 1.5 *Physical memory in multiprogramming*

1.5 Time-Sharing Systems

As is the case with the batch systems, the user cannot interact with the job when it is being executed. It would pose serious problems when dealing with multistep jobs, in which case the output of one step may be necessary for the successful completion of another job and so on.

To counteract this problem, *time-sharing* systems were introduced. Time-sharing can be viewed as an extension of multiprogramming. The CPU executes number of jobs by switching between them.

The frequency of these switches is so high that the user can interact with each program at any time during its execution.

In interactive computer systems, the users can directly interact with the system. The user can type a command at the prompt, see the output and basing on the output he may type another command. A text editor to enter and modify the programs using keyboard and a debugger to assist the user in debugging his programs have been the common features in today's interactive computer systems.

Using a time-shared operating system several users can share the computer *simultaneously*. Within the time a user types a command, the CPU switches so rapidly that each user feels as if he had his own computer. But, actually, only one CPU attends to the jobs of all the users *simultaneously*.

The time-shared operating systems are even more complex than the multiprogrammed operating systems because, while designing these systems, many features like memory management, protection, job synchronization and many more should be incorporated.

The concepts *multiprogramming* and *time-sharing* form the main theme behind the presently available operating systems.

1.6 Multiprocessor Systems

The advent of very large scale integration techniques and other developments in the electronic industry have brought into existence the *personal computer*, known more famously as PC. As the cost of the hardware decreased, each user can get a computer system completely dedicated to him.

If a processor takes 1 msec to execute a specific job,

how much time would two identical processors working together on the same job take? Obviously, they take less than 1 msec. This analysis is the basis for the invention of *multiprocessor* systems.

If one processor executes one job in a unit of time, *n* processors cannot execute *n* jobs in the same amount of time, however. That number would be less than *n*. This decrease is a direct result of the contention for shared resources and the pressure in maintaining all the *n* processors function correctly.

Using these multiprocessor systems greater reliability can be obtained. If one of a set of *n* processors fails then each of the remaining processors will share its workload, which results in the improvement in the reliability of the overall system.

1.7 Distributed Systems

The distributed systems form another variety of computer systems. These are the systems with each system having its own memory and processor. The sizes and functions of all the processors in these systems need not be the same. They may vary. The advantages provided by these systems include resource sharing, communication and computation speedup etc.

1.8 Real-Time Systems

A *real-time* system is a specific purpose system. This is, in general, used to control the speed of operation of a processor or the data flow etc. in a dedicated application like undersea exploration, robotics etc.

A real-time system consists of fixed and clear-cut time constraints. For smooth functioning of the system processing must be done within these constraints.

There are two types of real-time systems: *hard real-time systems* and *soft real-time systems*. Hard real-time systems guarantee the completion of critical tasks on time. Here, every delay needs to be bounded. Many essential features of a general-purpose operating system are absent in real-time operating systems. These are most widely used in industrial control and robotics.

Soft real-time systems have relatively relaxed time constraints. Here, a critical task gets priority over others and that priority continues until it completes. These systems are used in virtual reality and multimedia etc.

So far, we have examined all types of computer systems from simple batch systems to complex real-time systems. It is now time to define an operating system.

1.9 What is an Operating System?

An operating system is an **interface** between the computer and the user. It provides an environment where the user can make **efficient** use of the hardware and execute his programs in a **convenient** manner.

An operating system is an essential part of almost every computer system. When one is working with a computer, he is working with an operating system.

The operating system provides a means for making the best use of the resources, namely software, hardware and data. To be frank, an operating system does not do any useful function on its own. It just provides an environment where the users can carry out their tasks conveniently and efficiently.

An operating system can work efficiently as a resource allocator. It allocates the resources of a computer system like CPU time, I/O devices etc. to various programs and users.

An operating system can also function as a control program to control the execution of user programs to avoid errors.

An operating system can also be defined as a program that runs at all times on the computer.

1.10 Layers of an Operating System

An operating system is a very complex piece of software

that offers a lot of functionality to the user. It is a proven strategy to organize the operating system into a set of a layers rather than a single program. This layered approach offers modularity. The heart of the operating system is known as *kernel* and it forms the first and central layer of the operating system. A great deal of the functionality provided by the operating system is handled by the kernel alone. The kernel is the only layer of the operating system that has the ability to talk to the underlying hardware in a computer system. It is one of the important duties of the operating system to hide the peculiarities of the hardware from the user. The operating system accomplishes this task with the help of *device drivers* that are a big part of its kernel. TCP/IP stack, file systems, memory managers and process managers etc. are among the other important parts of the kernel.

All the commands and application programs form the second layer. The command line interface and/or the windowing system form the third layer and the user directly deals with this layer. Figure 1.6 is a graphical representation of the layers of an operating system.

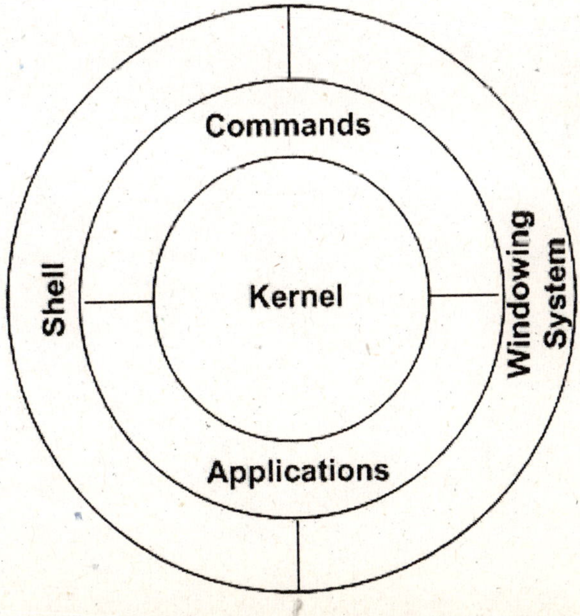

Figure 1.6 *Layers of an operating system*

Thus, this is a discussion on the history and evolution of operating systems. As we have seen in this chapter, operating systems and the computer architecture have influenced each other in a great deal.

Today, the availability of highly versatile operating systems made it very easy for us to make the best use of hardware in an efficient manner. To further improve the ease of operation of the system, a lot of research is still going on in this field, of course.

Review Questions

1. What is an operating system?
2. Explain in detail the concept of batching
3. Batching could improve the CPU utilization to a good extent. Justify.
4. Explain how human involvement was eliminated in job sequencing.
5. What is meant by spooling?
6. Spooling is a good concept to make the CPU and I/O work at faster rates. Explain.
7. What is multiprogramming?
8. How can several users make use of the services of a single CPU simultaneously?
9. The switching rate of the CPU is very high in a time sharing system. Why?
10. What are different types of real time systems?

CHAPTER

2

Computer System Structures

Introduction

The main aim of this chapter is to help the reader review the basic concepts of the structure of a computer system. As said in the previous chapter, the main purpose of the operating system is to control all the I/O devices. Also, the operating system has a very close tie-up with the I/O mechanisms. Hence, this chapter begins with a discussion on I/O.

One of the very important duties of the operating system is to ensure correct functioning of the entire system. The proper functioning of the system protects the operating system and other user programs as well as their data from any malfunctioning program. These issues are studied in the latter portion of this chapter under the title 'hardware protection'. The computer can accomplish its job of executing the programs only when they reside in the main memory. But the main memory is limited in size. Hence, the computer systems make use of the secondary storage. A considerable portion of this chapter is devoted to studying about the storage structure.

2.1 I/O Structure

In this section, the principles of I/O hardware are discussed first. Then the I/O software is studied.

2.1.1 Device Controller

The set of I/O devices and device controllers in a computer system make up the I/O hardware. Each I/O device is controlled by what is called a 'device controller'. That means the device controller acts as the supervisor of the devices that are connected to it. Depending upon the type of the device controller the number of devices it can control varies.

A device controller takes the form of a printed circuit board that can be fixed in a specific slot on the motherboard. The operating system always deals with the device controller but not with the devices directly. The bus model shown in figure 2.1 is used in all mini and microcomputers.

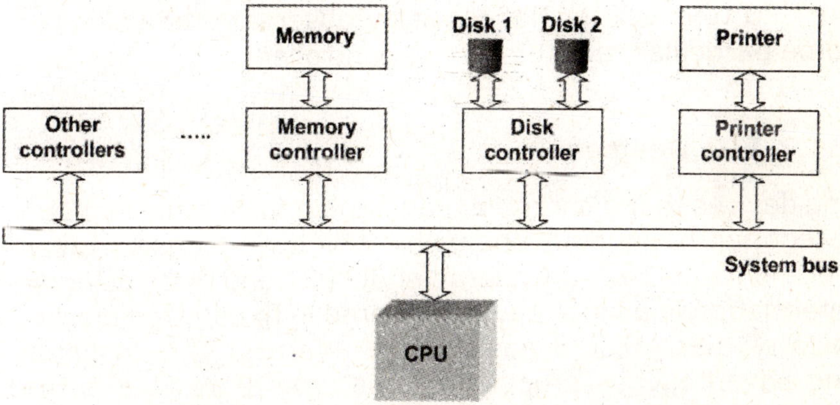

Figure 2.1 *Bus model of controllers*

The CPU interacts with the devices through the device controller. The device controller maintains some buffer storage that can hold the data from the devices it controls. The size of this buffer is a dependent of the type of the device being controlled. The data stored in this buffer is converted into a block of bytes by the controller. Also, if any errors are found they are corrected.

The controller maintains some registers also, which are used to communicate with the CPU. These registers are used by the operating system to write the I/O commands.

The number of instructions that a device controller can accept varies from one controller to another. The common commands that many controllers can accept are READ, WRITE, and COPY etc. Many of these commands have parameters.

The operating system loads the registers of the controller with appropriate values of these parameters. The job of the operating system finishes once it loads the controller registers properly. Then the controller does the rest. It controls the functioning of the device and once the task is accomplished it makes an interrupt and thus allows the operating system to regain the control of the CPU. The operating system then checks the results of the operation.

Again, the controller registers play their role by containing the output of the operation. The operating system directs the CPU to check for the result by observing the values in some particular registers of the controller.

2.1.2 I/O Devices

The devices that a controller can handle fall mainly into two categories depending upon how the data transfer takes place in them. They are character devices and block devices. Information in a block device is stored in fixed-sized blocks. Each of these blocks has its own address. The essential and advantageous property of this type of devices is the possibility to read or write any block independent of others. An example of block devices is disks.

On the other hand, in character devices, information is sent or accepted in streams of characters. Examples of character devices are line printers, punched cards etc.

The devices can be categorized into different groups basing on their speed, data representation, the type of operations they perform and their error handling methodologies.

2.1.3 Direct Memory Access

Direct memory access or DMA is the property by which the controller is allowed to access the memory directly and the CPU is freed from the low-level work of reading the data from the controller's internal buffer and writing it into the main memory.

When DMA is not used, the controller reads an entire block into its internal buffer. Then it computes the check sum to verify whether any read errors have occurred. Next it causes an interrupt. And, eventually, the CPU reads this block of data from the internal buffer of the controller into the main memory. As is evident, a lot of CPU time is wasted in this process.

When DMA is used, the controller is given a total of 3 items of information: the disk address of the block, the main memory address where this block is to be copied, and the count of the bytes to be transferred. The DMA address and the count are stored in two separate registers in the controller.

After the controller completes reading the first block of information from the device it verifies the check sum and then writes this block into the address specified in the 'DMA address register'. Then it increments the DMA address and decrements the DMA count by the number of bytes transferred. This process repeats as a loop until the DMA count becomes zero. Once the count becomes zero the controller causes an interrupt.

2.2 Principles of I/O Software

The purpose of software is to hide certain peculiarities of the hardware from the user and to provide an easy-to-use interface to operate the hardware. It is because of the properly developed software that we are able to get the printout of a piece of text or a graphical image just with a mouse click. We do not bother about what is happening inside once the 'OK' button is pressed.

As said earlier, properly developed software provides a clean and regular interface to the users by achieving its goals like device independence, uniform naming and error handling etc. An efficient way of achieving these goals is to structure the I/O software in different layers. Each of these layers performs specific tasks. For instance, the device drivers issue commands to the drive registers and check that they are carried out properly. And, the functions of device independent software include device naming, error reporting and buffering etc.

2.3 Storage Structure

The CPU can execute any program only when that program and the data being used by that program are on one of the direct-access storage devices. These direct-access devices include the main memory and the registers built into the CPU. If the data needed is not in these memory areas it must be moved there.

But, as said earlier, this total memory is less in amount and hence many computer systems make use of the secondary storage devices, which are non-volatile in nature.

2.3.1 Disks

Today almost all computer systems use magnetic disks for storing information. The main advantages of magnetic disks over main memory are:

- They possess much larger storage capacity.
- The price per bit is comparatively less because the recording density, defined as the number of bits recorded in a unit area, is more.

The structure of a disk is simple. Both the surfaces of the disk platter are covered with magnetic material on which information is stored. The disk surface is logically divided into tracks, which are further divided into sectors. Information is recorded in these sectors.

As the surface area of the disk increases, the number of concentric tracks and hence the number of sectors increases. Although the sectors close to the outer rim of

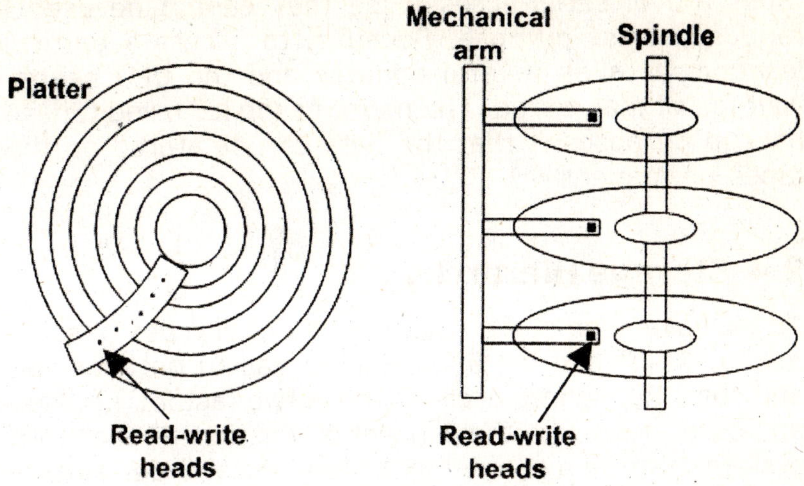

Figure 2.2 *Disk structure.*

the disk are physically longer than those close to the hub, each sector contains the same number of bits.

Hard disks and floppy disks are the most commonly used disk types. The storage capacity of hard disks is many times greater than that of floppy disks. The capacity of currently available hard disks is more than 120 gigabytes, whereas that of floppy disks is 1.4 Mbytes. High-density zip disks are also available presently.

Magnetic disk is also one type of device. Hence its working is governed by a device controller, which is known as disk controller. The disk controller accepts instructions from the CPU and orders the disk drive to execute those instructions. Also, the disk controller maintains some local buffer to hold the data recently written to or read from the disk.

Optical disks are yet another type of disks. These disks make use of lasers to store information. These are slower than the magnetic disks but are more rugged and less costly. Also, these disks have the added advantage of removability.

2.3.2 Magnetic Tapes

Magnetic tapes also provide a secondary storage medium, which is mainly used for back-up purposes. Since these tapes are of serial-access type they cannot be used for random access purpose. Because, to access a particular location, it takes several minutes and the CPU needs to wait for all that period. The main reason for using tapes for backup purposes is that the data can be stored on these tapes permanently.

2.4 Storage Hierarchy

As we have seen so far, there are several types of storage media, which can be differentiated basing on their speed and cost. Taking into account these two factors, i.e., speed and cost, along with the concept of volatility all the storage systems can be arranged in a hierarchical order as shown in figure 2.3.

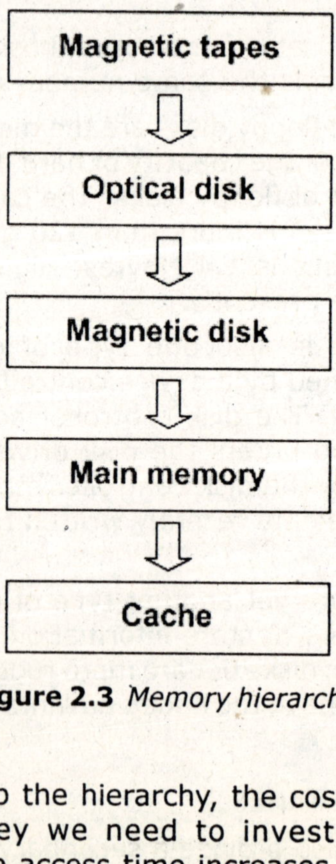

Figure 2.3 *Memory hierarchy*

As we move up the hierarchy, the cost per bit i.e., the amount of money we need to invest to store a bit, decreases but the access time increases. That means the data in the main memory is readily accessible but the cost to store that data there will be more.

As can be observed, we cannot use a single type of storage system in any computer system. Instead, a combination of more than one system is what is used in general.

For example, consider the personal computer many of us are using presently. As we know, there appear main memory (RAM), hard disk, floppy disk, and cache in any typical PC. Each of these storage systems is used for a specific purpose.

2.5 Hardware Protection

The research endeavours of scientists in their fields will no doubt bring out a better, simple and convenient system. However, such a system cannot be completely free from the side effects. And the field of computers is no exception to this truth.

In the early days of computing, there used to be single-user, programmer oriented systems. The programmers had control over the entire system. Hence, if any error occurred the programmer would make corrections for it. Later, operating systems were developed to free the programmer from arranging the jobs in a sequence - the job sequencing was made automatic.

Afterwards, to improve CPU utilisation, time sharing systems were developed and the concept of multi-programming was introduced. These new concepts, of course, offered several advantages to the user but parallelly they introduced several problems as well.

For instance, a bug in one program can affect many processes in a time-shared system and an erroneous program might change the data or code of another program in a multiprogrammed system. These problems can more or less be eliminated if the following hardware facilities are provided:

- Proper Interrupt Mechanism

- Dual-mode Operation
- Memory Protection
- Real time clock

In this section, we will study each one briefly.

2.5.1 Interrupt Mechanism

A program under execution might face an interrupt, which might make the CPU attend a particular interrupt service routine that starts from a specific memory location. In order that the interrupted process continues executing correctly, the memory location where from the CPU jumped to attend the interrupt must be noted by some mechanism. In the presence of such an interrupt mechanism the following sequence of actions takes place when an interrupt occurs:

The CPU

- Pushes the value in the instruction pointer on the top of the stack.
- Loads the instruction pointer with the starting address of the interrupt service routine.
- Jumps to the new address.
- Executes the ISR.
- And, upon coming across the RETURN statement in the ISR, loads the IP with the value on the top of the stack.
- And, continues executing the interrupted process.

2.5.2 Dual-Mode Operation

By making the hardware run in 2 modes, the *supervisor mode* and the *user mode* we can protect the operating system and other programs from any malfunctioning program.

The user programs are run in the user mode and the privileged instructions are executed in the supervisor mode. When an attempt is made to execute the privileged instructions in the user mode the hardware traps to the operating system.

The main drawback of this mechanism is that a process has all or no privileges at any time. For example, a process executing in the supervisor mode enjoys all the privileges irrespective of whether it needs them or not.

Similarly, a process executing in the user mode might need some essential privileges, which it doesn't currently hold. To manage this problem, the idea of the *domain of protection* is introduced. A domain defines a set of privileges that a process executing in it can enjoy.

A process must need to jump to another domain if it wants to make use of certain other privileges. Of course, these transitions from one domain to another are strictly controlled by the operating system.

2.5.3 Memory Protection

When there are several processes executing concurrently, we must protect the memory used by one process from unauthorized and illegal access by another process. This protection is achieved with the help of the base and limit registers. These 2 registers help in determining the range of legal addresses that the program can access.

The base register holds the smallest legal physical memory address and the limit register carries the size of the range. If, for example, 15000 is the value in the base register and 4500 is contained in the limit register then the program can access all the memory locations from 15000 to 19500 inclusive.

2.5.4 Real Time Clock

Timers are used to interrupt the user processes after a specific period of time. This method is very useful in that it prevents the user processes from not returning the control to the operating system. The operating system returns the control to the user process only after ensuring that the timer is set.

Another significant use of timers is to implement the concept of time-sharing. Each user is allowed to make use of the CPU to execute his programs until the time-slice allocated to him expires. Once this time-slice expires, the operating system allots the CPU to another competing user. This allocation is done making use of certain scheduling policies, which are discussed in a later chapter.

Review Questions

1. What is a device controller?
2. A device controller acts as a medium through which the CPU interacts with the devices. Explain.
3. What is the purpose of registers in a device controller?
4. What is the main difference between block devices and character devices?
5. Explain DMA.
6. In what way DMA is advantageous?
7. What is the advantage of structuring the software in layers?
8. What are the advantages of magnetic disks over main memory?
9. Explain the structure of a disk.
10. All the sectors have identical storage capacity. Justify.
11. What is the function of a disk controller?
12. Although magnetic tapes are sequential in nature they are used as secondary storage devices. Why?
13. Explain the storage hierarchy.
14. What is 'cost per bit'?
15. Explain how the CPU responds to an interrupt call?
16. What is dual mode operation?
17. How can illegal accesses to memory be avoided?

CHAPTER

3

Operating System Structures

Introduction

This chapter discusses what services are provided by an OS, how they are provided, what factors are to be taken into account while designing an OS, what is the user's view of an OS etc.

Let us begin our discussion with the following description.

Suppose that we are planning to construct a house. Then how do we start? Exactly! We begin with a *plan*. The first step in preparing such a plan is to decide the number of rooms the house should consist of. Say, we want to build a house consisting of one kitchen, two bedrooms, one dining hall, and one drawing room. Then, the second step is to decide what features each room should have. Then we hire an architect and start the process of constructing the building. In a crude sense, a building is said to be ready when all its components, i.e., rooms, are constructed and the interconnection between them is provided. A house is nothing but a collection of several rooms connected to each other, after all.

Exactly the same pattern is followed in the development of operating systems also. At first, we think about the different services we want the operating system to provide.

Then we develop different components to offer these services. After successful completion of this step we logically connect all these components and thus the operating system with the required features is ready.

In this way, an operating system can be viewed as a set of software programs. Now let us see what the components of a typical operating system are.

3.1 Operating System Components

There are four major components that are present in most of the presently available operating systems:

- Process Management
- Memory Management
- Information Maintenance
- Protection and Security

And also, a few other components like networking and command interpreter system play a good role in evaluating the efficiency of an operating system in providing numerous services to the user. Below is a brief description about each of these components.

3.1.1 Process Management

A process, in simple terms, is a program under execution. Consider a multiuser system where there will be several processes competing for the allocation of resources like CPU. If it is a uniprocessor system, there will be only one instruction pointer and other registers. So, the operating system has to keep track of all the competing processes, schedule them, and run them one after another. The services to be provided under this process management are as listed below:

- Creation and termination of user and system processes.
- Changing the priority of a process.

- Suspension and resumption of a process.
- Blocking a process.
- Provision of some means for process synchronization and deadlock handling.
- Delaying a process.

3.1.2 Memory Management

Corresponding to the two forms of memory there are two different memory management schemes.

- *Main-Memory Management:* As it has been said earlier, any program to be executed must be loaded into the main memory. For improving the utilization of the CPU, as many programs as possible should be loaded into the main memory. In this regard, the operating system is supposed to perform the following activities:

  ¤ Maintain a list of available parts of memory.

  ¤ Allocate and deallocate memory to different processes.

  ¤ Schedule the processes to bring them into the main memory when the memory becomes available.

  ¤ Keep track of the memory blocks being used.

- *Secondary Storage Management:* As we know, the main memory is volatile in nature. That means, whenever the power is off all the data in the main memory is lost. Hence, we need to back up the data in the main memory on to the secondary storage devices like magnetic disks. In the presently available PCs hard disks are used to store software like compilers, assemblers and debuggers etc. until they are loaded into the main memory.

3.1.3 Information Management

This refers to a set of services used for storing the

information, retrieving it or deleting it. This component deals with the organization of information in terms of directories and files, allocating and deallocating the sectors to various files. The services that result under this management are:

- Creation and deletion of files.
- Creation and deletion of directories.
- Opening and closing a file or directory.
- Taking backup of files on secondary storage media.
- Changing presently working directory.
- Reading data from a file to buffer.
- Writing data from buffer to a file.

Information management is also known as file management.

3.1.4 Protection and Security

A system may have several users and hence several concurrently running processes. Hence, it becomes necessary to protect the various processes from the illegal activities of the users. For fulfilling this requirement, various mechanisms are designed whose ultimate goal is to make sure that the resources like CPU, memory segments are allocated to only those processes with proper authorization.

Protection, which refers to the mechanisms for controlling access to programs or processes, improves the reliability of the system to a great extent.

3.1.5 Networking

Networking refers to the phenomenon of interconnecting several processors, as a result of which the user at one position would be able to access the information at a remote site, provided he has proper authentication. The operating system takes care of all the problems and complications that arise as a result of this interconnection.

3.1.6 Command Interpreter System

A command interpreter system is the most important system program of an operating system. It acts as an interface between the user and the operating system. In user-friendly operating systems like Windows and Macintosh, the user will be able to open a file or directory, invoke a program etc. by clicking the mouse placing on the appropriate icon.

In relatively complex operating systems, the user has to type commands at the prompt and press the Enter key in order to get his command executed.

3.2 Operating System Services

To study the services an operating system provides is yet another interesting task. Before that let us see a small description:

Suppose you want to deposit your money in a bank. Then you would consult the bank manager and open an account with the bank. Then your name along with your details will be noted in the central registrar of the bank, which contains the details of all its customers. Suppose that you have gone to the bank some day to withdraw some amount. Then the clerk you have approached would refer to your details like your specimen signature, balance in your account etc. and he will do the needful. Then you will be issued a withdrawal form and your name will be noted in the list of customers served that day.

While your work is being processed if any other person comes he would need to wait until the clerk becomes free to serve him. After the clerk becomes free he attends that person.

This is exactly what an operating system does. With this backdrop one can easily understand the following description about the services of an operating system.

- The user writes his programs in files. He may want to delete a particular file when he no longer needs it. The operating system must provide a means to *create and delete files by name*.

- After writing a program the user may want to execute it. The operating system must be able to load that file into main memory and execute it. The operating system must provide a means to *correct the mistakes if any*.
- The operating system should make a provision to *allow two or more processes to communicate with each other*.
- The operating system must be able to *control the I/O devices*. For example, consider the case when you want to print a text file stored on the hard disk.
- The operating system should act as a *resource allocator*. In an environment, where there are many users with multiple jobs trying to make use of the available computer resources concurrently, the necessity to schedule their jobs or processes to allocate them the resources arises.
- The operating system must also provide security to the files of the users in a multiuser computer system. There should be some means to make sure that the users' processes do not get interfered with one another or with the operating system. The *access to all the system resources should be controlled*.
- The operating system should maintain a record about the users using the resources. This would be helpful for the researchers for several purposes.

3.3 System Calls

A system call is an interface between the operating system and the process. These system calls are available as assembly language instructions. However, today several high level languages like C allow the processes to make system calls directly.

Whenever a system call is made, the preparatory instructions generated by the compiler load certain registers with the parameters of the system call. For example, if we want to read the contents of a file *XYZ*, the required system call may be *OPEN*, say. The actual appearance of the system call with the parameters specified would be as follows:

OPEN *XYZ R*

Here *XYZ* and *R* are the parameters, where *XYZ* is the name of the file and *R* indicates the mode, which stands for 'read'.

There are five major categories of system calls:

- Process job management
- File management
- Device management
- Information management
- Communications

3.3.1 Process Management

A program being executed should be able to *end up* either normally or *abort* abnormally. This abnormal termination comes whenever there are bugs in the program. A process executing a specific program may require the output of another program to end up the execution of this first program. Hence, there should be the provision to *load* and *execute* that second program.

We may even want to *create* a process, *terminate* a process, and *get the attributes* of an already existing process. We may *set the attributes* of a process - we may change its priority, for example.

All these come under the process management.

create process, terminate process
load, execute
end, abort
Get process attributes, set process attributes

Figure 3.1 *System calls under the process management category*

3.3.2 File Management

Consider the case when you want to type some text in a file. Then you need to *open* an empty file, type/*write* into it, *save* it, and then *close* it. Similarly, you may want to *read* the contents of a file. You may even write at the end of the existing file i.e., you may want to *append* to it. All these system calls come under the category of file management.

The same set of calls may be needed for manipulating directories also if the file system is organized into directories.

open, close
read, write, append
save
delete

Figure 3.2 *System calls under the file management category*

3.3.3 Device Management

This block includes system calls made by different files to access certain devices like a printer, speaker etc. For example, if we want to *print* the contents of a text file, we need to *request* the printer. We have to ensure that the printer is ready i.e., it is turned ON. Then we check for the sufficiency of the paper. After our job is complete we *release* the printer.

request device, release device
read device, write device
get device attributes, set device attributes

Figure 3.3 *System calls under the device management category*

3.3.4 Information Maintenance

This block consists of system calls used for maintaining a continuous flow of information between the user and the operating system. We may want to know the system *date* and *time*. System calls exist to know the *list* of files in the system and also to know the number of processes being executed. Provisions are also there to know how many users are currently making use of the resources, the available memory etc.

We can also access the information relating to a particular file or directory like - what is the name of that file, when is that file or directory is created, when is it modified, what is the size of that file and so on.

3.3.5 Communications

Two processes on the same computer or on different computers may want to communicate with each other. Before the communication between these two processes takes place, a connection must be opened. The system calls *get host id, get process id, open connection, close connection* serve to establish and close connection between two processes. Once the connection is established the client and server can send and receive messages.

get host id
Get process id
open connection, close connection

Figure 3.4 *System calls under the communications category*

So far, we talked about the operating system absolutely from the programmer's point of view. We said that the operating system would consist of several system calls and it would offer several services.

Now let us see the same concept from a different perspective i.e., from the user's point of view.

A common user is always concerned about what he is typing at the console and what output he is getting. He does not care about system calls or any other complex operating system features.

3.4 User's View of the Operating System

Generally, a user communicates with the computer by typing some commands at the command prompt. The operating system consists of a program known as *command interpreter* that runs constantly in the computer. This CI interprets the commands of the user, produces corresponding output and waits for the next command to be entered. This concept is the basic idea behind *event driven programming*. In case of windowing environment, along with keyboard interaction the user can use mouse movement, mouse clicking etc. to drive events.

Thus, the operating system is a set of CI commands from the user's point of view. Every CI command will have one or more programs associated with it. The CI also consists of a watchdog program along with these programs.

Assume that in an example the CI contains 3 commands namely *CRT* (to create a file), *DEL* (to delete a file) and *RUN* (to run a file). Whenever a user types a command at the command prompt, the watchdog program checks whether such a command is there in the list or not. If the command is found the executable program identified by this command is loaded into memory and executed and the result is displayed and then the prompt appears again. If that command is not available an error message is displayed and then the prompt appears so as to enable the user to type in another command.

Now let us see how the algorithms of the command routines work. Consider the following example in which a user wants to run a program named *XYZ*. This program is already compiled, linked and stored in the hard disk. The sequence of steps is as follows:

- The prompt appears on the screen and the cursor blinks indicating that the system is ready.
- The user then types the command *RUN XYZ* and presses Enter key.
- As soon as he presses the Enter key, the command is transferred to the buffer of the command interpreter.

- The watchdog program then checks whether the command *RUN* is valid or not.
- If it finds it to be a valid one the file name (*XYZ* in this case) is passed as a parameter to the *RUN* program.
- The *RUN* program, using a system call belonging to the Information Management block, locates the file *XYZ* and finds out its size.
- Now, using another system call belonging to Memory Management block, the *RUN* program checks whether there is sufficient memory available in the active memory to accommodate that program. If there is not enough memory error message will be displayed and the work is terminated.
- If memory is available then with the help of a system call belonging to IM block that program is loaded into the active memory.
- Then the access rights of the user are checked. That means, it is checked whether or not the user has the right to execute the program.
- If the user had the right the *RUN* routine, with the help of a system call in the process management, schedules that program and eventually executes it.

Thus, it is evident that the system calls belonging to different categories will have to work in close association with one another.

3.5 System Design and Implementation

So far, we have seen in depth the features of an operating system and the services it should provide. Now, in this section, we will discuss the issue of designing and implementing a system.

3.5.1 Steps in Designing the System

In this part, one needs to specify the type of the system i.e., whether the system is batch, time-shared, single-user or multiuser etc. Later, the properties of the system need to be specified. The user, in general, may want the system to be fast, reliable, flexible and efficient.

The next step is to determine the policies and mechanisms. Policies determine what should be done on a particular occasion and mechanisms determine how it should be done.

After we are satisfied with our requirements and specifications the task of implementing the system needs to be undertaken.

3.5.2 Implementation

Traditionally, operating systems were written in assembly language. But today high-level languages are used to implement the systems. Although high-level languages are less efficient in some aspects (like their requirement for more memory and their low speed etc.), they have their own merits:

- The code produced using a compiler can be made more efficient by recompiling it with another good compiler
- An operating system written in high-level language is easier to port. For example, if an operating system is written in assembly language on a specific CPU, it can be used only on that system. But the operating systems written in high-level language can be used on any system having any CPU. For example, UNIX, written in C language, can be used on any system.

After the system is coded it needs to be configured to work on a specific machine. For configuring this system there will be a special program. During configuring the system this program notes the details of the hardware system like:

- The type of CPU
- Available memory
- Available I/O devices etc.

With the help of these details the operating system can be made ready to work on that machine. After an operating system is installed the hardware must be enabled to use it. But how does the hardware know where the operating system is stored in memory and how to load it. These questions are worth answering and hence the following description about *kernel* and *booting*.

3.5.3 Kernel

The operating system is very complex software consisting of several routines. Hence, the size of this software would be more. So it is not wise to keep the entire software in the active memory always, as the working area would be less. Hence, the operating system is divided into two parts. The first part contains the very essential routines, which are very often required and the other part consists of relatively less frequently used routines. The first part is known as Kernel. Whenever the system is switched ON, this kernel gets loaded. The remaining programs and routines are loaded as and when are necessary.

3.5.4 Booting

How the operating system is loaded? As we have said earlier, the operating system is responsible for all the I/O operations. Then how can the operating system be loaded into the memory? Who will load it? We cannot say a particular program loads it into the memory because, in order to be executed that program should be brought into the memory, which is the duty of the operating system.

The answer goes like this: In many systems, the operating system is stored on the ROM, which is nonvolatile in nature. This should be brought into the active or volatile memory whenever the system is switched ON. In these systems, the ROM contains a minimum program to which the control is transferred immediately when the computer is switched ON. This program loads a special program known as BOOT from the boot sectors. This boot program then loads the kernel. This process is known as bootstrapping process or simply booting. Once the kernel is loaded it takes care of the rest of the functionality.

Review Questions

1. What are the different components of an OS?
2. What are the different services rendered by an OS?
3. What is a system call?
4. In how many classes can the system calls be categorized?
5. What is the user's view of the operating system?

CHAPTER

4

Process Management

Introduction

This chapter, which starts with the definition of *process*, extensively discusses the topics process states, process control block, process scheduling and operations on processes. A brief theory about *threads* is also presented at the end of this chapter.

Let us begin with the definition of the term *process*. A process is defined as something that competes for computer resources like CPU etc. Then, can we call a program a process? The answer is 'No', because a program on the hard disk is equivalent to that written on the paper. The only difference is that it is typewritten and compiled. In order to execute the same, it needs to be loaded into main memory and exactly at that point of time it is called a process. So, a process can be defined as **a program under execution, which competes for computer resources**. The concept of *process management* is about scheduling the multiple processes that are in the active memory, keeping track of various processes.

4.1 Process States

The state of a process waiting in the memory changes

several times before the process completes executing. This change of state is the result of CPU's *switching* among several processes. Each process may be found in one of the following states at any time:

- *New:* This state indicates that the process is created.
- *Running:* In this state, the process gets its instructions executed.
- *Ready:* A process which is not waiting for an I/O or which is not running is said to be in ready state. It is a state just before the running state. A process in this state is waiting for the CPU to be allocated to it.
- *Blocked:* When a process is waiting for an external I/O operation to be performed, it is said to be in the *blocked* or *waiting* state.
- *Terminated:* This state indicates that the process has finished its execution.

4.1.1 Context Switching

The registers of the CPU maintain important information about the process currently executing. When a process moves out of running state its context has to be saved so that it can later resume its execution correctly. Once the CPU becomes free it will be allocated to another process by the CPU scheduler. That means the CPU makes a switch between two processes. During switching, the CPU will first save the context of the process moving out and then it updates its registers with the context information of the process that is scheduled to run.

4.2 Process State Transitions

- When a process is created the operating system keeps it in the list of new processes.
- When there is room for this process it is put into the ready queue. It remains in the queue until the CPU becomes ready to serve it.

- When the turn of this process comes the operating system dispatches it to the *running* state by updating the registers.
- Like all the other processes, this process is also given a time slice. Before this time slice expires the process needs to complete its execution. Otherwise, it will be again put into the *ready* state.
- If the currently running process needs to wait for I/O, the operating system blocks that process and puts it in *waiting* state and dispatches another process in the ready state to the *running* state. Once the I/O operation is complete, the process blocked becomes eligible to be brought into the ready queue where it has to compete for the CPU again.
- This cycle repeats until the process is terminated.
- After termination, the process is put into the terminated or halted state and then all its details are removed from the active memory.

Figure 4.1 is a schematic representation of what is described above.

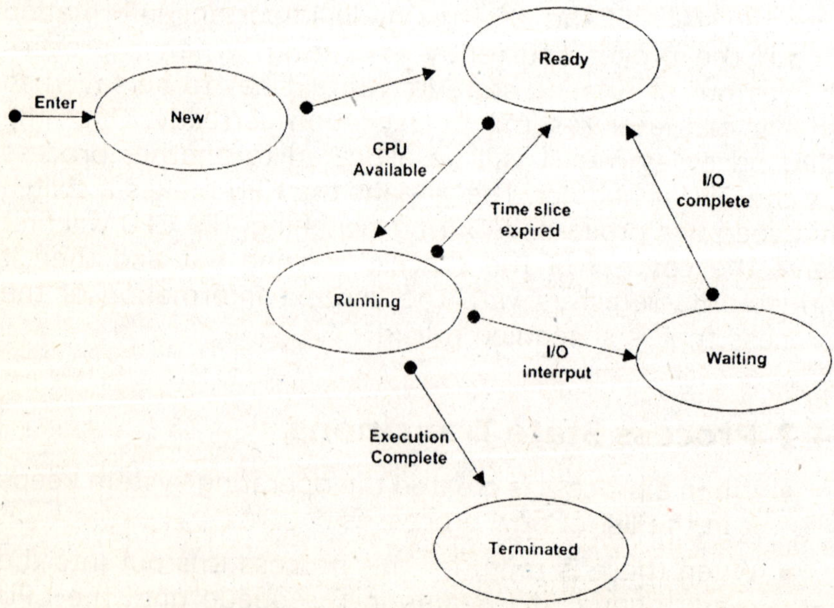

Figure 4.1 *Process state transitions*

4.3 Process Control Block

The information about each process is maintained by the operating system in a record known as Process Control Block (PCB). This block is created when a user creates a process and is deleted from the system when that process is terminated. The memory reserved for the operating system is generally used for maintaining all the PCBs. The fields within a PCB are:

- *Process-id:* This is the number given by the operating system to a process when it is created. A process is always addressed using its id. If the operating system can handle a total of *n* processes, it gives numbers to the processes from *0* to *n - 1*. If $(n + 1)^{th}$ process is created then the operating system gives it the number *0* assuming that the 0th process created earlier has already been terminated.
- *Process State:* This field gives the current state of the process. It may be any of *Ready*, *Running*, *Blocked* etc.
- *Process Priority:* The user may externally set a higher priority to a process than the others. In some systems the operating system will do this internally. A high priority process always gets the CPU before a low priority one.
- *Program Counter:* This is a register that contains the address of the next instruction to be executed for this process.
- *Scheduling Information:* This field consists of pointers to scheduling queues and any other scheduling parameters.
- *Accounting Information:* This gives the account of the usage of the computer resources (CPU time, connect time etc.) by different users so that they can be charged.
- *List of Open-files:* This gives the list of all the files that are opened for the process. These files automatically get closed when the process terminates. Otherwise, the operating system will close them.

Process id
Process state
Scheduling info.
Registers (PC)
Pointers (to memory, scheduling queues etc.)
List of open files
Accounting info.
Other info.

Figure 4.2 *PCB*

- *Other Information:* This may include the details like the path of the presently working directory. This may also include some more useful information maintained by the operating system.

4.4 Process Scheduling

- *Goals of scheduling:* When there are many processes running concurrently in the system, some form of scheduling is necessary to control the access to the CPU by different processes. The main objectives of scheduling are fairness and increased throughput (the number of processes completed per unit time)
- *Different scheduling queues:* Whenever any process is created, it is put in the *job queue*. This queue contains all the processes in the system. When the turn of a process comes it is loaded into the memory and is transferred to another queue known as *ready queue*.

When a process is executing it may need to do I/O. Hence it enters, quitting the CPU, into another queue known as *device queue* or *I/O queue*.

When a process is executing one of the possible events are:

- The process may enter the I/O queue making an I/O request.
- The CPU may remove the process when the time slice expires and put it on ready queue.
- The process may need to create another child process and wait until it terminates.

This information is clearly depicted in figure 4.3, which is known as queuing diagram.

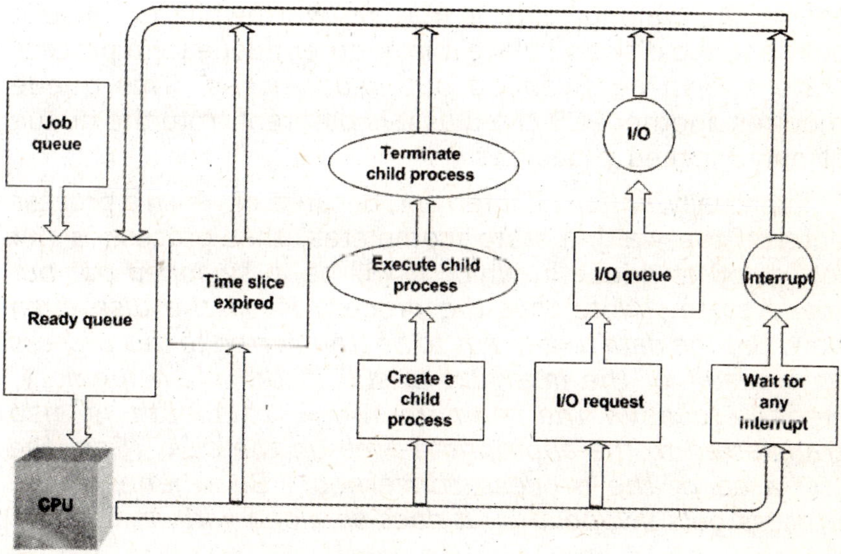

Figure 4.3 *Queuing diagram*

4.4.1 Scheduling Levels

There are 3 different levels at which the operating system can schedule the processes. They are:

- Long-term scheduling
- Medium-term scheduling
- Short-term scheduling

An operating system can use one or any combination of these 3 levels subject to the sophistication required.

In a batch system, the number of processes submitted is usually far greater than the number of processes that can be executed. All these processes are stored on a disk at the time of submission. Now, the job of long-term scheduler is to select the processes from this pool and put them into the ready queue.

Because of memory problems it is sometimes advantageous to decrease the degree of multiprogramming (the number of processes executing simultaneously). So whenever a process is blocked i.e., whenever any process enters the waiting state it may be worthwhile to swap it out on to the disk and place it in another queue for a process state known as *swapped out and blocked*. This queue requires another PCB chain as it is different from the queue of only blocked processes.

Eventually, when the interrupt, because of which a process entered the waiting state, completes, that process is put into another queue in which it will be in *swapped out but ready* state. *[Note that the process is on the disk even now. But the data that needs to be transferred to this process as a result of the interrupt is still in the main memory. Hence, to save the main memory, this data is also transferred to the appropriate area on the disk. (Say, the I/O area of the process concerned.) So whenever the process gets swapped in, it does so along with its data.]*

The medium-term scheduler takes care of all these steps.

The third scheduler is the short-term scheduler or CPU scheduler. The purpose of this scheduler is to select one process from the ready queue and allocate the CPU to it.

4.5 Operations on a Process

Below a list of common operations on processes is provided.

Almost all of these operations result in the change of state of the processes. The *process-id* (pid) is supplied as the parameter to all of these system calls.

The general operations performed on processes are:

- Create a process
- Kill a process
- Block a process
- Wake up a process
- Dispatch a process
- Change the priority of a process
- Time up a process

4.5.1 Process Creation

A process, while getting executed may create one or more new processes using the *create_process* system call. The process created is known as the child process. (It is the child of the parent process).

The child process may have access to the computer resources in two ways:

- It may have to use a part of the resources of its parent.
- It may be allocated the resources being treated as a separate process by the operating system.

In general, the former approach is followed by several systems because it prevents any process from overloading the system by creating too many sub processes.

When a process creates a new process two possibilities may result:

- The parent may execute concurrently with the child process.
- The parent may wait until the child process is terminated.

4.5.2 Process Termination

The process terminates when it finishes executing its final instruction. The operating system then deallocates all the resources to this process.

The case of a process having a child process is of special interest. In general cases, the child process also terminates in a fashion similar to that of its parent. In some special cases listed below, the parent process may abort the child process.

- The child may be trying to make use of the resources exceeding the limit.
- The parent process may be exiting and the operating system may not allow the child process to continue.

The remaining operations on processes are self-explanatory, which could be implemented using various system calls.

4.6 The Concept of Threads

We can define a process by the resources it uses and by the location where it is getting executed. It is always advantageous if the resources are shared and accessed concurrently. The mechanisms using threads support this concept. A thread is a lightweight process.

Each thread has a program counter, stack and register save area. But it shares the *same address space* with others. A thread shares its code and data sections with its *peers*.

In many aspects, threads act in a similar way as processes do. They can be in one of *ready*, *running*, *blocked* or *terminated* states. Like processes, threads can also share the CPU and, at any given time, only one thread is running. Like processes, threads can also create child threads and abort them when necessary.

The only difference between threads and processes is that threads are not independent of each other. A user can own an individual task that contains multiple threads. These threads cooperate with each other.

The reason why the concept of threads became so popular is the richness of advantages it provides.

- The overhead involved in creating a new thread in an existing process is very less.
- The overhead involved in terminating a thread is also very less.
- The switching between two threads within a process occurs very quickly.
- Asynchronous elements in the program can be easily implemented as threads.
- Using multiple threads the speed of execution of a task improves very much.
- Complex programs can be easily designed and implemented using threads.

Another important point to note is that some actions like swapping affect all the threads simultaneously. It is because of the reason that all the threads share the same address space and operations like swapping move the entire address out of memory.

Although multithreaded approach offers numerous advantages, it has never been a universally accepted technique to code complex applications. This is chiefly because of the struggle involved in debugging multithreaded programs. Even experienced programmers find it hard to code and debug multithreaded applications.

Multithreaded programming is hard because threads share 'too much'. And, it is a hard requirement to coordinate access to shared data with locks. This requirement must *always* be met. If the programmer forgets to lock or unlock a mutual exclusion variable, which guards a critical section of code from getting modified parallelly by more than one thread, the result would be disaster.

There is a famous suggestion in the field of systems programming to *forget thinking about multithreading a program if somebody is paying for the work*. And, now we know why it is true.

4.7 Cooperating Processes

All the processes executing simultaneously could be divided into two categories:

- Independent processes
- Cooperating processes

If a process does not share any data with any other process, it is an independent process. On the other hand, a cooperating process is a process that affects other processes and in turn gets affected.

This process cooperation is very important as it provides the following advantages:

- *Increased computation speed:* In a multiprocessor system a task may be divided into several subtasks and all the subtasks must be run concurrently to increase the speed of computation.
- *Provision to share information:* In a multiuser system, several users may access a common (shared) file concurrently.
- *Ease of operation:* A single user may work on several processes at a time.

The concept of cooperating processes can best be illustrated with the help of *producer-consumer* problem. The consumer consumes the information that has been produced by the producer. The producer process communicates with the consumer process with the help of a shared variable where the data is stored.

The producer process and the consumer process need to be synchronized in order to prevent the latter from trying to consume an item that has not yet been produced.

4.8 Interprocess Communication

The IPC facility provides the means for the cooperating processes to communicate with each other and to

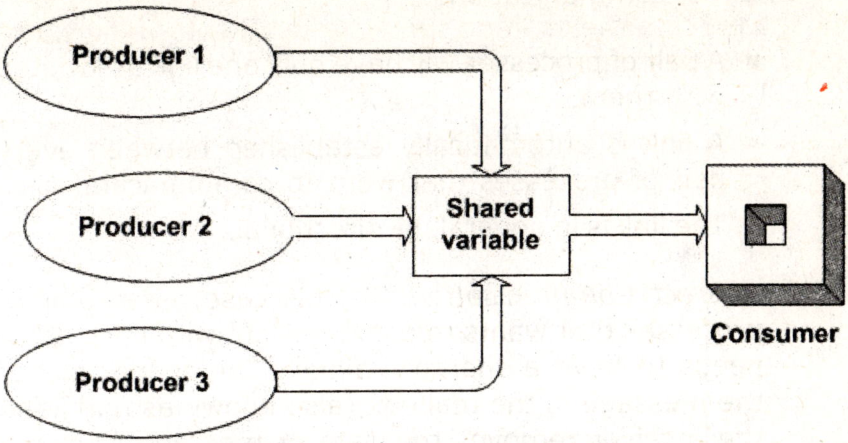

Figure 4.4 *Producer-Consumer processes*

synchronize their actions. Interprocess communication is best provided by a message system.

The key idea behind IPC is *message passing*. That means, one process sends a message and the other process receives it. So the message system should provide at least two operations: *send message* and *receive message*.

For any two processes to communicate with each other a link must be established between them. This link may be unidirectional or bi-directional. Also, the messages can be of fixed size or of variable size.

The link between two processes can be implemented using direct communication or indirect communication disciplines.

- *Direct communication:* Here the process that wants to communicate with another process must explicitly state the name of the sender or receiver. The send and receive primitives in this case are defined as follows:

  ¤ *Send (A, message):* Send a message to process A.

  ¤ *Receive (B, message):* Receive a message from process B.

In direct communication:

- ¤ A pair of processes will have only one link associated with them.
- ¤ A link is automatically established between every pair of processes that want to communicate.
- ¤ The link is in general, bi-directional.

- *Indirect Communication:* In this case, each pair of processes that wants to communicate with each other needs to have a shared mailbox. The sender places the message in the mailbox (also known as port) and the receiver removes the data or message from the box. In this case, the send and receive primitives are defined as follows:

  - ¤ *Send (P, message):* Send a message to mailbox P
  - ¤ *Receive (Q, message):* Receive a message from mailbox Q

In indirect communication:

- A link is established between a pair of processes only if those processes have a shared mailbox.
- A link can be associated with more than one pair.
- A link may be either unidirectional or bi-directional in nature.

Depending upon the number of messages that can be stored inside a link temporarily, its capacity can be assessed as zero, finite or infinite. That means, a link may not allow any or it may allow some or infinite messages to reside inside it depending upon the requirements.

The role of the message system in a distributed environment is of special interest. In such an environment, different processes lie on different machines and the communication between them takes place with the help of transmission lines. In this case, the probability of occurrence of mistakes is high.

For instance, a message may be lost because of an error in the hardware of the communication link, or because the sender process or receiver process terminates before the message is processed or because the message reaches the destination completely scrambled. In all these cases, the operating system may check for these errors and make corrections for them.

Review Questions

1. Define a process.
2. What are the different states that a process may enter during its execution?
3. How does the transition from one state to another occur?
4. What information is contained in a process control block?
5. What is the necessity of process scheduling?
6. What are the goals of process scheduling?
7. What are different scheduling levels?
8. What are the operations performed on a process?
9. Explain how threads make up a useful concept?
10. What are cooperating processes?
11. Explain interprocess communication.
12. What is direct communication between two processes?

CHAPTER

5

Processor Scheduling

Introduction

Processor scheduling is the main key to multiprogramming. In the previous chapters, we have seen that the CPU utilization increases considerably when the CPU has always some process to work for. In a uniprocessor system, when there are more processes, each has to wait until the currently running process completes executing and relinquishes the CPU. (Of course, sometimes, when the process needs to do I/O or when the time slice allocated to it expires, the process may need to quit the CPU though it did not execute completely.)

CPU is one of the major computer resources. Scheduling the CPU is very important and is central to the design of the operating system.

The CPU scheduler or the *short-term* scheduler selects one process from a pool of many to allocate the CPU to it. The dispatcher then deallocates the CPU to the currently running process and allocates it to the newly selected process. The delay between the stopping of one process and the starting of another process is known as *dispatch latency*.

The CPU scheduler may make decisions

- When the process switches from *running* state to *halting* or *blocking* state.
- When the process switches from *running* state to the *ready* state or *blocking* state to the *ready* state.

In nonpreemptive scheduling, the currently running process cannot be forced to quit the CPU. Processes competing for the CPU must wait until the currently executing process voluntarily releases it. On the other hand, in preemptive scheduling, a high priority process can *preempt* the running process and gain access to the CPU.

5.1 Scheduling Criteria

Scheduling criteria are helpful in choosing a particular scheduling algorithm.

- *Response Time:* It plays an important role in interactive systems. It is the interval between the time of submission of a request and the time when the response is observed. For example, when we type a command at the prompt the response time is the time from the moment we press the Enter key and the moment when the output is observed.
- *Turnaround Time:* It is appropriate for a batch system. It is the time interval between the time of submission of a process and its completion. It includes the actual execution time plus the time spent in ready and output queues.
- *Predictability:* Regardless of the burden on the system a typical process should always finish executing in the same amount of time and at the same cost. It is a user-oriented criterion.
- *Throughput:* It is a measure of the amount of work done by the CPU in a unit time. It should be as high as possible to increase the utilization of the CPU.
- *Waiting Time:* It is the main criterion affected severely by the scheduling algorithm. It is the sum of the periods of time spent in the ready queue.

- *Fairness:* Unless any external guidance compels, all the processes should be treated the same and no process should suffer starvation.
- *Enforcing Priorities:* When priorities have been given to some processes the scheduling policy should favour the processes with higher priority.
- *Processor Utilization:* It is the percentage of time the processor is busy. It is a significant criterion for expensive systems.

5.2 Different Scheduling Algorithms

In this section, a few important scheduling algorithms are explained.

5.2.1 FCFS (First Come First Served) Algorithm

It is the simplest scheduling algorithm. As the name suggests, the process that requests the CPU first is allocated the CPU first. When a process newly enters the ready queue its PCB is linked at the tail of the queue. The process at the head of the queue is allocated the CPU immediately when the CPU becomes free.

The main disadvantage of this algorithm is the longest waiting time. A typical process has to wait for a long time for the CPU to be allocated to it.

Let us study this algorithm with the help of an example. The table given in figure 5.1 lists four processes with corresponding CPU burst times (given in milliseconds).

Process	CPU Burst Time
P1	19
P2	6
P3	3
P4	1

Figure 5.1 *Processes with different CPU burst times*

Say, these processes arrived in the ready queue and hence served in the order P_1, P_2, P_3 and P_4. Then, using the Gantt chart given below, we see that process P_2 waits for 19 msec, P_3 for 19 + 6 = 25 msec, and P_4 for 28 msec. As is evident, it is a drawback of this algorithm to make the process (P_4) with a burst time of only 1 msec wait for 28 msec.

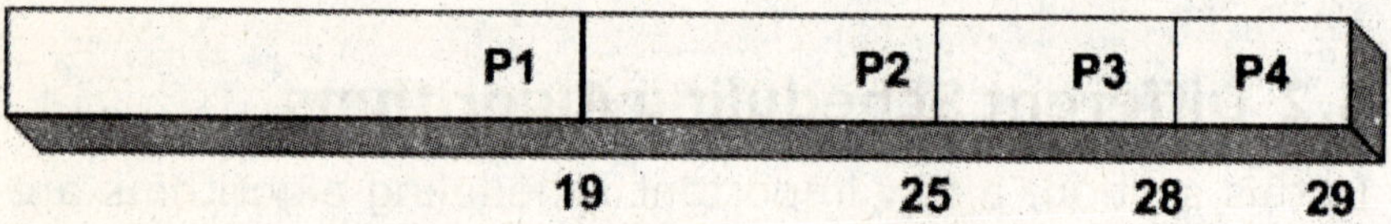

Figure 5.2 *Gantt chart for FCFS*

Here, the average waiting time is (19 + 25 + 28) / 4 = 18 msec. Figure 5.3 shows what happens if the processes arrived in the order P_4, P_3, P_2 and P_1.

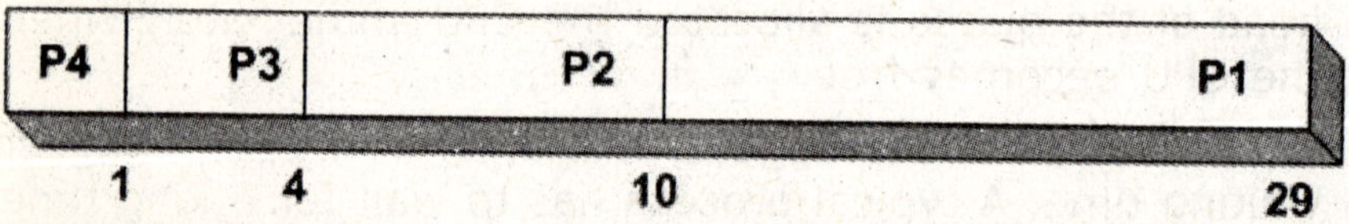

Figure 5.3 *Gantt chart for FCFS (when processes arrive in a different order)*

In the second case, the average waiting time is (1 + 4 + 10) / 4 = 3.75 msec (approx.). Hence, we can conclude that the sequence in which the processes enter the ready queue severely affects the average waiting time. FCFS algorithm is nonpreemptive. The main advantage of this algorithm is it is very easy to implement.

5.2.2 SJF (Shortest Job First) Algorithm

Here, each process is associated with the length of the next CPU burst of the next process. When the CPU becomes free it is allocated to the process with the *shortest next*

CPU burst time. This algorithm is optimal in that it gives the minimum average waiting time for a set of processes. This algorithm can be either preemptive or nonpreemptive.

Consider the set of processes shown in figure 5.4 as an example. In brackets are given the arrived time of each process. This time is used only for preemptive scheduling. In nonpreemptive scheduling, it is assumed that all the processes have arrived at the same time.

Process (arrival time)	CPU Burst Time
P1(0)	4
P2(1)	2
P3(3)	5
P4(5)	7

Figure 5.4 *Processes with different arrival times*

Nonpreemptive: Here, the Gantt chart will be as shown in figure 5.5.

Figure 5.5 *Gantt chart for non-preemptive SJF*

Here, the average waiting time is (2 + 6 + 11) / 4 = 4.75 msec.

Preemptive: In the preemptive scheduling, the arrival time is also taken into account. The Gantt chart for the example given above will be as shown in figure 5.6.

Here, the process P_1 is allocated the CPU first. It is preempted after 1 msec because the process P_2, which arrives at this time, has relatively short CPU burst and hence

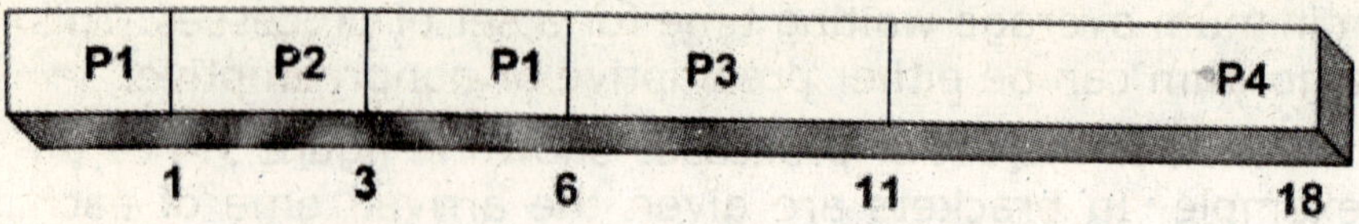

Figure 5.6 *Gantt chart for preemptive SJF*

it is allocated the CPU then, which it retains until it completes executing. After it is executed, the CPU is allocated to the process P_1, which requires two more milliseconds of CPU time. Like that, it continues. In this case, the average waiting time is given by (2 + 0 + 3 + 6) / 4 = 2.75 msec.

The main problem with this algorithm is the difficulty in implementing it at the level of short-term CPU scheduling because there is no way to find out exactly the next CPU burst of a particular process. We can just predict it. This algorithm is used in long-term scheduling.

5.2.3 Priority Scheduling

In this algorithm, a priority is attached to each process. The process with highest priority is given the CPU first. In case of a tie, FCFS algorithm is used. It can be either preemptive or nonpreemptive. Consider the following set of processes as an example.

The Gantt chart gives:

The average waiting time is (10 + 29 + 35) / 4 = 18.5 msec.

Process	CPU Burst Time	Priority
P1	10	1
P2	6	3
P3	19	2
P4	1	4

Figure 5.7 *Processes with different priorities*

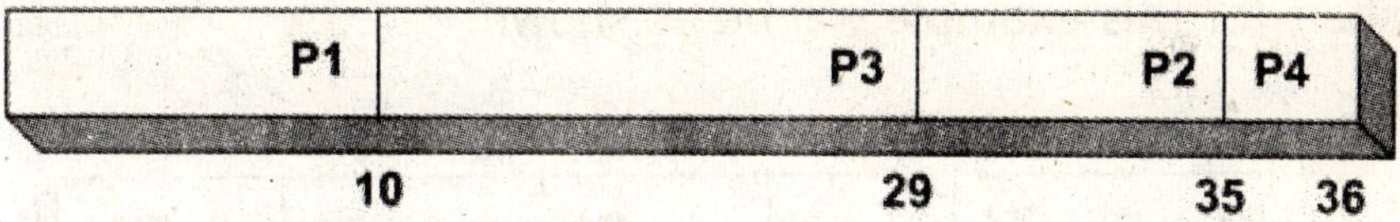

Figure 5.8 *Gantt chart for priority scheduling*

The main disadvantage of this algorithm is that it may cause the processes with low priority to suffer from indefinite blocking or starvation. That means, the process with low priority may need to wait in the ready queue for indefinite time for the CPU to be allocated to it. This problem is called starvation. The remedy for this is *aging*. Aging refers to the process of increasing the priority of the process that has been waiting in the ready queue for a long time.

5.2.4 Round Robin Scheduling

In this type of scheduling, a time slice known as *time quantum* is defined for every process. If the process completes executing before the quantum expires it voluntarily releases the CPU. Otherwise, it will be preempted and the CPU will be given to the next process in the ready queue. In this scheme, the ready queue is implemented as a *first in first out* queue. That means, every new process entering is added at the tail of the queue.

Process	CPU Burst Time
P1	19
P2	5
P3	3

Figure 5.9 *Processes with different CPU burst times for RR*

Consider the following example. (Assume that all the processes arrived at time 0)

Say, the time quantum is of 5 msec magnitude. The Gantt chart for this example will be as shown:

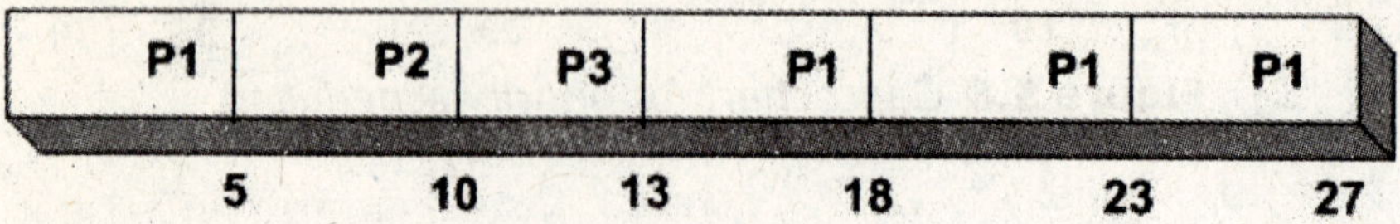

Figure 5.10 *Gantt chart for RR*

At first, the CPU is allocated to P_1. It retains the CPU for the scheduled time i.e., 5 msec. And then, process P_2 is allocated the CPU. It gets completely executed in the time quantum assigned to it. Then process P_3 gets the CPU and it too completes executing within the time slice allocated. Then, process P_1 again gets the CPU and completes executing in successively allocated slices of time.

The average waiting time in this example is (8 + 5 + 10) / 3 = 7.67 msec.

The FCFS scheduling is equivalent to RR scheduling with a very large time quantum.

If the time quantum is very small, the CPU needs to make several context switches thereby wasting much of its time in switching.

5.2.5 Multilevel Queue Scheduling

This is a special type of scheduling, which partitions the ready queue into several separate sub queues. Depending upon some properties of the processes, for example priority, they are permanently assigned to various queues.

We may implement different scheduling algorithms in different queues. If the processes are placed in different queues depending upon their priorities, all the processes in the queue with the highest priority are executed first and then the next queue (the queue in the second position of priorities) is given the CPU and so on. That means the queue with the least priority will be allocated the CPU last. In order to prevent the problem of starvation, we can use time slicing. Here, each queue is given the CPU for a certain amount of time. This time slice is then distributed among various processes in the queue.

Here, we have seen that the processes are permanently assigned to a particular queue upon their entry. They cannot move between the queues.

Using multilevel feedback scheduling we can enable the processes to move between the queues. Here also the processes are placed in various queues basing upon their priority and each queue is given a time slice.

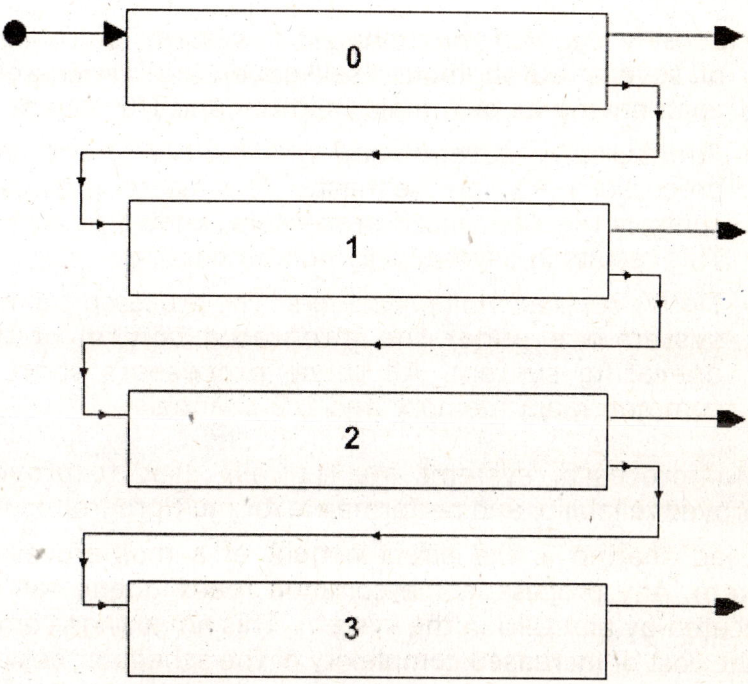

Figure 5.11 *Multilevel feedback queues*

If a process in one queue fails to complete executing in the time slice given to it, it will be placed at the tail of the next queue. If there are no processes in a queue, the process at the head of next queue is given the CPU. Similarly, if a process has been waiting for a long time for the CPU to be allocated, it will be moved into a higher-priority queue.

This algorithm is most general scheduling algorithm that can be configured on any system.

5.3 Multiprocessor Scheduling

Our discussion so far has concentrated on systems with only one processor. In this section, we will be studying briefly about scheduling in systems having more than one processor.

Basically, multiprocessor systems can be classified as follows:

- *Loosely coupled microprocessor system:* It consists of several autonomous (self-governing) processors, each having its own main memory and I/O channels.
- *Functionally categorized processors:* Here one processor will act as the master. This master processor controls the specialized processors, known as slaves. This results in asymmetric multiprocessing.
- *Tightly coupled multiprocessors:* The processors in this system are under the integrated control of the operating system. All these processors share a common main memory and I/O channels.

Multiprocessor systems are typically used to provide improved reliability and performance for multiprogramming.

Load sharing is the direct benefit of a multiprocessor system. Any process in the common ready queue can be executed by any CPU in the system. This advantage comes at the cost of increased complexity of the scheduler design.

5.4 Real-Time Scheduling

We have already discussed about real time systems in chapter 1.

Real time computing can be defined as that type of computing whose correctness depends mainly on the time at which the results are produced. A *hard real time task* must meet its deadline, failing which undesirable damage or fatal error may be created in the system. On the other hand, a *soft real time task* also has a deadline, which is desirable but not mandatory.

In hard real time systems, every process is submitted along with a note of how much time it takes. If the scheduler can make the process execute within that time period, it accepts that process. Otherwise, the process will be rejected since time is the main criterion in hard real time systems. The complexity of the software systems to run the hard real time systems is really great and they lack the full functionality of a typical operating system.

On the other hand, soft real time systems can be built with the help of carefully designed scheduler and other aspects. An important aspect of this system is that it must have priority scheduling and real time processes should receive highest priority. Most importantly, the priority of any process should not change at any moment of time.

5.5 Evaluation of Scheduling Algorithms

So far, we have studied about different algorithms. This section discusses various techniques to *evaluate* a particular scheduling algorithm.

5.5.1 Analytic Evaluation

Deterministic modeling is one type of analytic evaluation. This method evaluates a specific algorithm by comparing the efficiencies of different algorithms on a specific, predetermined workload. Consider the example shown in figure 5.12.

Process	CPU Burst Time
P1	8
P2	24
P3	2
P4	6

Figure 5.12 *Processes with different CPU burst times: analytic evaluation*

Our aim is to find out the best algorithm from FCFS, SJF and RR algorithms by calculating the average waiting time in each case.

FCFS algorithm: The Gantt chart in this case will be as shown in figure 5.13.

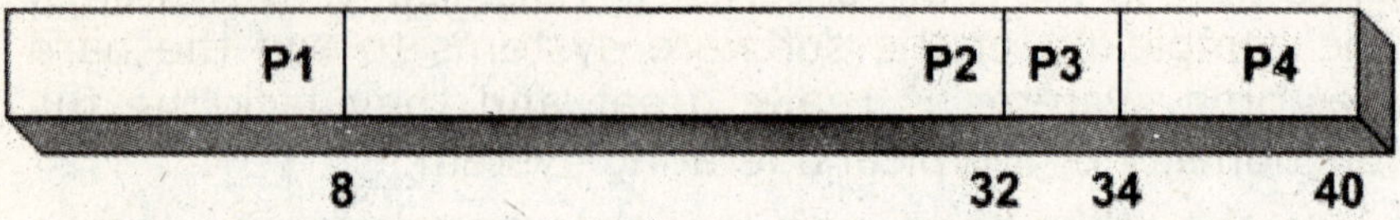

Figure 5.13 *Gantt chart for FCFS: analytic evaluation*

The average waiting time in this case is (8 + 32 + 34) / 4 = 18.5 msec.

SJF algorithm:

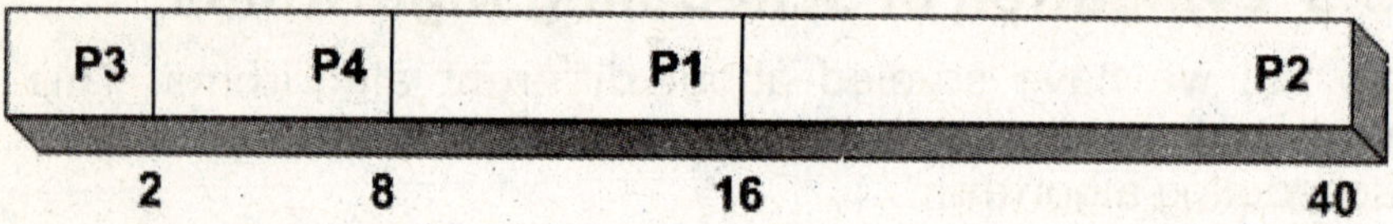

Figure 5.14 *Gantt chart for SJF: analytic evaluation*

The average waiting time in this case is (2 + 8 + 16) / 4 = 6.5 msec.

RR algorithm: (with a time quantum of 8 msec)

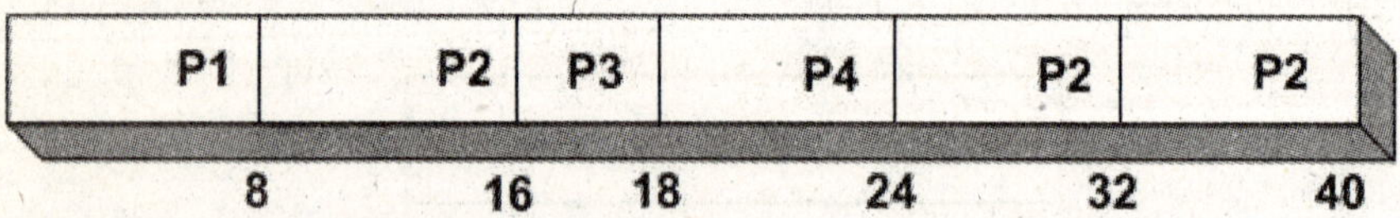

Figure 5.15 *Gantt chart for RR: analytic evaluation*

The average waiting time in this case is (0 + (8 + 8) + 16 + 18) / 4 = 12.5 msec.

Since the SJF algorithm results in only 6.5 msec of average waiting time, it can be evaluated as the best algorithm in this case.

This type of evaluation is very simple and fast. The main disadvantage of this evaluation method is that we may not know the exact details of all the processes.

Hence, we make use of a mathematical formula known as *Little's formula* to calculate the average throughput, utilisation and average waiting time. The details one has to know to make use of this formula are the arrival and service rates of processes.

If n is the length of the queue, w is the average waiting time in the queue and r is the arrival rate for new processes then $n = r \times w$ is known as Little's formula. If any two of the variables n, r and w are known, we can calculate the other variable. This type of analysis is known as queuing-network analysis. The drawback of this type of evaluation is that the arrival rates and service distributions cannot be determined exactly. Hence, we cannot trust the results obtained completely.

5.5.2 Simulations

Simulations provide relatively more accurate evaluation of scheduling algorithms. Here, we generate the data required for simulations in a number of ways. After the simulation executes, the statistics that indicate the performance are gathered and thus the efficiency of an algorithm is evaluated.

However, simulations often consume lot of money and also the time of computers. Moreover, we cannot rely upon the results completely. Also, it is really cumbersome to design, code and debug a simulator.

5.5.3 Implementation of Algorithms

The only way to evaluate the performance of an algorithm in an efficient and precise manner is to code it and put it in a real environment (operating system) and then observe its performance. However, this is a very costly approach. Also, the operating system may need to be changed to some extent to support the new algorithm.

In this way, there is no perfect way to evaluate the performance of any algorithm.

Review Questions

1. When does the CPU need to make decisions?
2. What are the criteria to select a scheduling algorithm?
3. Different processes and their burst times are given below. Illustrate the FCFS and SJF algorithms using the table.

Process	CPU Burst Time
P1	14
P2	7
P3	2
P4	4

4. What is preemptive scheduling?
5. What is priority scheduling? Explain with an example.
6. What is the main drawback of priority scheduling?
7. Explain round robin scheduling algorithm with an example.
8. What is the significance of time slice in RR scheduling?
9. How do you evaluate a scheduling algorithm?
10. What is the significance of Gantt chart?

CHAPTER

6

Deadlocks

Introduction

Deadlocks occur when two or more processes compete for non-sharable resources. A set of processes is said to be in deadlock state if every process in the set is waiting for an event that can occur *only* by another process in that set. To illustrate this, let us consider a system with only 2 printers each of which is held by two different processes. Now what happens if each process requests another printer? Yes, each has to wait until the other process releases the printer and hence they enter the deadlock state.

Deadlocks can also occur in the case of different resource types. For example, consider a system with one printer and one tape drive. Say, process P_A is having the printer with it and the tape drive is held by another process P_B. If process P_A requests the tape drive and process P_B requests the printer, what happens? A deadlock occurs because each process has to wait until the other process releases the requested resource.

6.1 Graphical Representation of a Deadlock

Deadlocks can be represented graphically. The conventions one needs to follow are given below:

- Each process is represented by a square.
- Each resource is represented by a circle.
- If a process is holding a resource the arrow will be from the resource to the process.
- If a process requested a resource and is not yet granted the same, then the arrow will be from the process to the resource.

Now consider an example. Assume that process P_a holds resource R_a and process P_b holds resource R_b. Now a deadlock is said to occur when the process P_a requests the resource R_a and process P_b requests resource R_b. The Directed Resource Allocation Graph given in figure 6.1 represents this case.

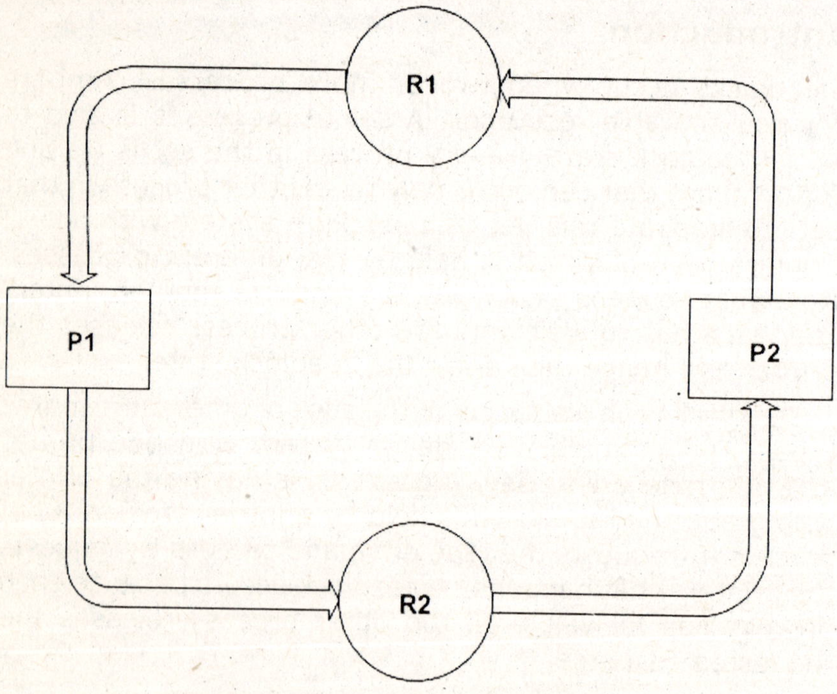

Figure 6.1 *Deadlock or circular wait*

6.2 Deadlock Prerequisites

A deadlock is said to occur when the following four conditions are satisfied:

- *Mutual Exclusion Condition:* At least one of the resources must be held in a non-sharable mode. That means, at any moment of time that resource can be held by only one process and the other processes need to wait for it until the presently holding process releases it.
- *Wait-For Condition:* Although a process presently holds a resource, it should be possible for it to request another resource with out releasing the one it already held resource.
- *No-Preemption Condition:* Until the process presently holding a resource releases it voluntarily, no other process should remove that resource from it forcibly.
- *Circular Wait Condition:* Processes $\{P_1, P_2, P_3 ...\}$ and resources $\{R_1, R_2, R_3 ...\}$ must form a circular chain such that P_1 is waiting for R_2, and P_2 is waiting for R_3 and so on. Figure 6.1 shows a condition in which deadlock is sure to occur. Process P_1 currently holds resource R_1 and is in need of resource R_2, which is currently held by process P_2. Also, process P_2 is waiting for resource R_1 to be free. This is a sure case of a deadlock since P_1 cannot release R_1 until it gets R_2 and finishes executing. Similarly, P_2 cannot release R_2 until it gets R_1 and finishes executing.

When all these four conditions are satisfied simultaneously, a deadlock will occur.

6.3 Deadlock Strategies

There are several strategies followed by different operating systems to deal with the deadlock problem. Some of them are listed below:

- Ignore the deadlock
- Detect it
- Recover from it
- Prevent it
- Avoid it

Here is a brief discussion on each of them.

6.3.1 Ignore a Deadlock

The simplest possible way to deal with the problem of deadlocks is to ignore it. Although it raises a doubt in one's mind, there are two reasons behind this motive.

Deadlock detection, prevention algorithms are very complex and are very difficult to code, test and debug.

Also, they make the system very slow. Hence, the users prefer a system with occasional deadlocks rather than a very slow, complex and restrictive system.

6.3.2 Detect a Deadlock

We may use DRAG to detect a deadlock. However, these DRAGs may sometimes elude the observer. The operating system has the following to be done in order to detect a deadlock.

- Give some numbers to all the processes like P_a, P_b ...
- Number each of the resources separately using a meaningful code.
- Maintain two tables: A resourcewise table and processwise table.

The resourcewise table should contain the details of the process to which it is allocated, its type etc. The processwise table should contain the details like the resources held by each process and the resource(s) it is waiting for. When a process releases a resource held by it both the tables should be updated.

Now with the help of these two tables, the operating system can detect whether a particular allocation could lead to a deadlock or not.

6.3.3 Recover From a Deadlock

Here two approaches are given to recover from a deadlock.

- *Suspend-Resume a process:* In this approach, a process having a low priority is suspended temporarily and the resources requested by it are allocated to another process (of course, to that having a higher priority). Later, when the turn of the suspended process comes it is resumed. Although this method seems somewhat fair, it is practically very difficult to implement it.

- *Kill a process:* If killing a process solves a deadlock, the operating system decides to kill a process with the lowest priority and that has just begun so that the loss that results is not heavy.

6.3.4 Prevent a Deadlock

In this strategy we take (preventive) measures by creating situations that will prevent a deadlock from occurring. In the previous section, we studied that a total of four conditions need to be satisfied for a deadlock to occur. Now, let us see how we can avoid these situations.

- *Mutual Exclusion Condition:* If we can make every resource in the system sharable then a deadlock would never occur. But unfortunately it is impossible. We may use a spooler in the case of printer resource to eliminate the need for sharing. But this spooling technique cannot be used with all other resource types.
- *Wait-For Condition:* If we can prevent a process that is presently holding a resource from requesting another resource we can prevent a deadlock from occurring.

  To achieve this, the operating system has to make it compulsory for every process to declare at the very beginning all the resources it is expecting to use. The operating system will allow this process to commence if and only if all the resources requested by it are available. The operating system, after allocating the resources, must update its list of free resources. Although this approach seems to be better, it is wasteful. For example, if a process does something for say six hours and at the end uses a resource for just one minute, the second resource has to be idle for a span of six hours and no other process can utilize it.

- *No Preemption Condition:* If we allow a process to remove a resource it wants forcibly from another process, it will give rise to worse problems although it solves the problem of a deadlock. One can easily imagine how worse the situation will be if a printer is made stop printing a document in the middle because another process forcibly removed it from the process that was currently holding the printer to print another document.
- *Circular Wait Condition:* So far, we have seen that attacking the first three conditions is very difficult. If this fourth condition is prevented we can prevent a deadlock.

  If each process is forced to hold only one resource at a time, the circular wait condition can be prevented. But this approach also has its own faults. For example, if a process P currently holds a resource R_1 and yet requests another resource R_2, it has to quit R_1 first and then only make a request for R_2. But the process may still be in need of R_1. So this is obviously a problem.

  There is an alternate approach. We may number each resource using a particular coding scheme and then force each process to request the resources in a predetermined sequence. However, the problem with this approach is that a process might not need the resources in the same order it is supposed to request. For example, using a specific coding scheme, consider that a process has a constraint to request for a printer first and then for a plotter and so on. What happens if the process wants a plotter first and then a printer? Obviously, it cannot get them. So this approach is also wasteful.

Hence, there is no universally accepted method to prevent a deadlock.

6.3.5 Avoid a Deadlock

To avoid a deadlock, the operating system follows a separate strategy. If a process requests for a resource, the operating system first allocates it to the process on the trial basis and checks whether such an allocation would result in a deadlock or not. If it doesn't, the resource is *actually* allocated to the process.

The most famous algorithm to avoid deadlocks is Banker's algorithm.

With the help of this algorithm one can know in advance whether a typical allocation could lead to unsafe state.

Banker's algorithm maintains dynamically two matrices. One matrix contains the details about resources that are already held by various processes. The other matrix contains the details about the resources that are required by the processes. Figure 6.2 illustrates this concept. Processes P_1, P_2 and P_3 are currently holding a total of 4 tape drives and 2 printers. And, they require 1 tape drive and 2 printers more. So, the total requirement for all the processes to finish executing successfully is 5 tape drives and 4 printers. If the total number of available resources is equal to or more than this requirement deadlock will never occur. Otherwise, deadlock may occur if certain conditions are met.

Process	Tape Drives	Printers
P1	2	1
P2	1	1
P3	1	0

Figure 6.2 *Matrix showing resources currently held by various processes*

Process	Tape Drives	Printers
P1	0	1
P2	1	0
P3	0	1

Figure 6.3 *Matrix showing resources still required by various processes*

The working of this algorithm is as follows:

- At the very beginning, each process declares all the resources required by it to the operating system. Then the operating system puts these figures in the second matrix.
- When a process requests a resource, the operating system checks whether the resource is free and whether that can be allocated. If the path is clear the operating system allocates that resource on a 'trial' basis to the process and updates the first matrix.
- Now the operating system checks whether this allocation creates any unsafe conditions. If there is no such problem, the operating system *actually* allocates that resource to the process that has requested it.

    Here, one needs to note that the 'unsafe' state does not mean a deadlock. It is just a situation of a potential deadlock. If a request made by a process results in an unsafe state then the operating system will postpone its decision to allocate the resource to that process.

According to the argument of the researchers it is not sufficient to use only one of the approaches (detection, prevention or avoidance) to deal with deadlocks. Hence, research is still going on to bring out an efficient approach, which is a combination of these three approaches.

Review Questions

1. How do deadlocks occur?
2. How can deadlocks be represented?
3. How can deadlocks be treated?
4. Ignoring a deadlock is the simplest strategy to follow. Explain.
5. How can deadlocks be prevented?
6. How can we avoid deadlocks?

CHAPTER

7

Memory Management

Introduction

We have concentrated in our discussion so far on processes that are in the main memory and competing for resources like CPU. Now, this chapter is about the ways to keep several processes in the main memory. That means we will be discussing about different approaches to *share* the memory.

The memory management systems can be divided into two major categories: *contiguous* and *non-contiguous*. In contiguous memory allocation scheme entire program will be loaded in contiguous (continuous) locations. On the other hand, the non-contiguous systems allow the program to reside in different portions of memory on being divided into different chunks.

Real memory management schemes demand the entire process image to be loaded into the main memory. On the other hand, virtual memory management schemes start executing a process even if only a part of the process is loaded into the main memory. Figure 7.1 lists different memory management schemes.

The issues that are involved in every memory management scheme are:

Real memory management systems

Contiguous:

Single contiguous memory management systems
Fixed partitioned memory management systems
Variable partitioned memory management systems

Non-contiguous

Paged memory management systems
Segmented memory management systems
Combined memory management systems

Virtual memory management systems

Figure 7.1 *Different memory management schemes*

- *Relocation and Address Translation:* At the compiling time the exact physical memory locations that a program would occupy at its run time are not known. The compiler compiles the program assuming that the program will be loaded from memory location 0000. At run time, the program may need to be relocated to different memory locations. And hence, the addresses may need to be changed.
- *Protection:* The memory management scheme should provide some measures to prevent one program from interfering with another program. Although the compiler has generated proper addresses and relocation is done properly, because of the malfunction of the hardware system the chance of one program interfering with another is there. Hence, protective measures are compulsory.
- *Sharing:* This is opposite in effect to protection. In some occasions, it should be made possible for multiple processes to refer to the same memory locations.
- *Evaluation:* There are a few norms like wasted memory, access time, and time complexity that we use to evaluate the efficiency of a typical memory management scheme.

7.1 Logical Address and Physical Address

The address generated by the CPU is known as logical address and the address seen by the memory unit is known as physical address.

A special hardware known as memory management unit does the mapping from logical address to physical address. The hardware contains a register known as *relocation register*, which holds a predetermined number. This number is added to the logical address generated by the CPU and the result is the physical address.

The set of all logical addresses is known as logical address space. And the set of all physical addresses is known as physical address space. This is illustrated in figure 7.2.

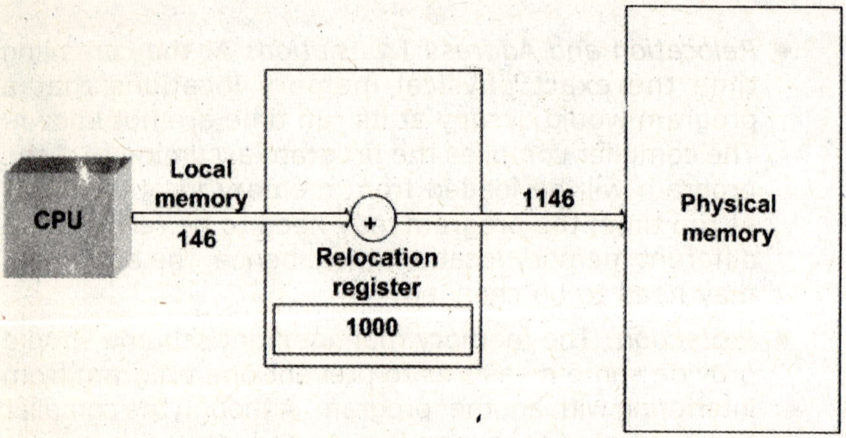

Figure 7.2 *Dynamic relocation*

7.2 Swapping

We have discussed about swapping very briefly in one of the previous chapters. Swapping is a good technique to deal with the *insufficiency* problems. If a running process enters the blocking state for some purpose, say, for I/O, it will be temporarily swapped out on to a disk (backing store) and the CPU will be allocated to another process. When all the processes executed, this process will be swapped in. If address binding is done at assembly or load time then the process that was swapped out of memory could be swapped into the same memory locations. However, if execution time binding is used the process would be swapped into another memory location because, in this scheme, addresses are computed only at run time.

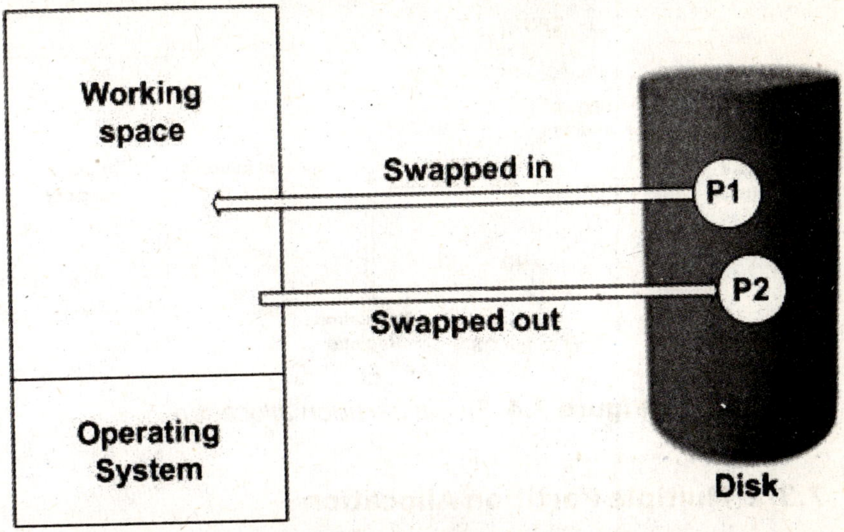

Figure 7.3 *Swapping*

7.3 Contiguous Allocation Scheme

In this scheme, the physical memory is divided into two contiguous areas, one part of which is permanently assigned to the operating system. The operating system can reside either in the lower part of the memory or in the upper part.

7.3.1 Single Partition Allocation

The hardware support for implementing this scheme includes a relocation register and a limit register. The *relocation register* contains the starting address and the *limit register* contains the limit of addresses. The logical address generated by the CPU is checked against the value in the limit register. If the address is less than the limit it will be added to the starting address in the relocation register to give out the physical address. Since each address generated by the CPU is checked (against the value in the LR) we can protect the users' programs from being changed by the running processes.

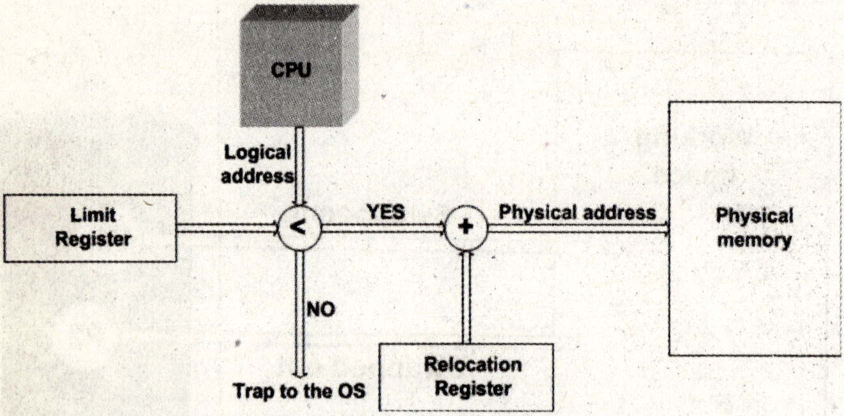

Figure 7.4 *Single partition allocation*

7.3.2 Multiple Partition Allocation

One of the simplest possible ways to distribute the available memory among the processes waiting in the input queue is to divide the available memory into some partitions of fixed size so that each partition contains only one process. When a partition is free one of the processes waiting in the input queue is allocated that block.

When a process requests memory the operating system searches for a block that is large enough to accommodate that process. If one is found, it is allocated to that process. The operating system always maintains a table to keep track of presently available blocks and the blocks that are currently in use. After each allocation the operating system updates the table.

Now consider an example:

Imagine that a total of 2500 K of physical memory is available and five processes P_1, P_2, P_3, P_4 and P_5 with certain individual memory requirements are waiting in the input queue. Suppose that the operating system occupies 400 K. Then 2100 K of user space is available. The following table gives the description of each process.

The net requirement of memory for all the processes is 2900 K. But the available memory is only 2100 K. Hence, the processes P_1, P_2 and P_3 are allocated the memory and

Process	CPU Burst Time	Required Memory
P1	9	500K
P2	4	800K
P3	21	400K
P4	8	700K
P5	5	500K

Figure 7.5 *Processes with different memory needs*

thus 300 K of memory is still available. But this is not sufficient for either P_4 or P_5. This distribution is as shown in figure 7.6A.

After four units of time process P_2 expires releasing 800 K of memory. This block can accommodate process P_4. Hence, P_4 is allocated it. Now the picture will be as shown in the figure C. After some time process P_1 expires releasing 500 K of memory and then this chunk of memory is allocated to P_5. This picture is as shown in figure E.

Here the allocation is done depending upon one of the *first fit*, *best fit* and *worst fit* algorithms.

7.3.3 External and Internal Fragmentation

External fragmentation exists when sufficient memory to satisfy a request exists but is not contiguous. In figure A, 400 K of external fragmentation is there. This memory space is not sufficient to cater to the memory needs of either P_4 or P_5. In figure C, there is a total external fragmentation of 100 K + 400 K = 500 K. This space is sufficient for process P_5. But it could not be allocated because the space is not contiguous. This goes into the account of

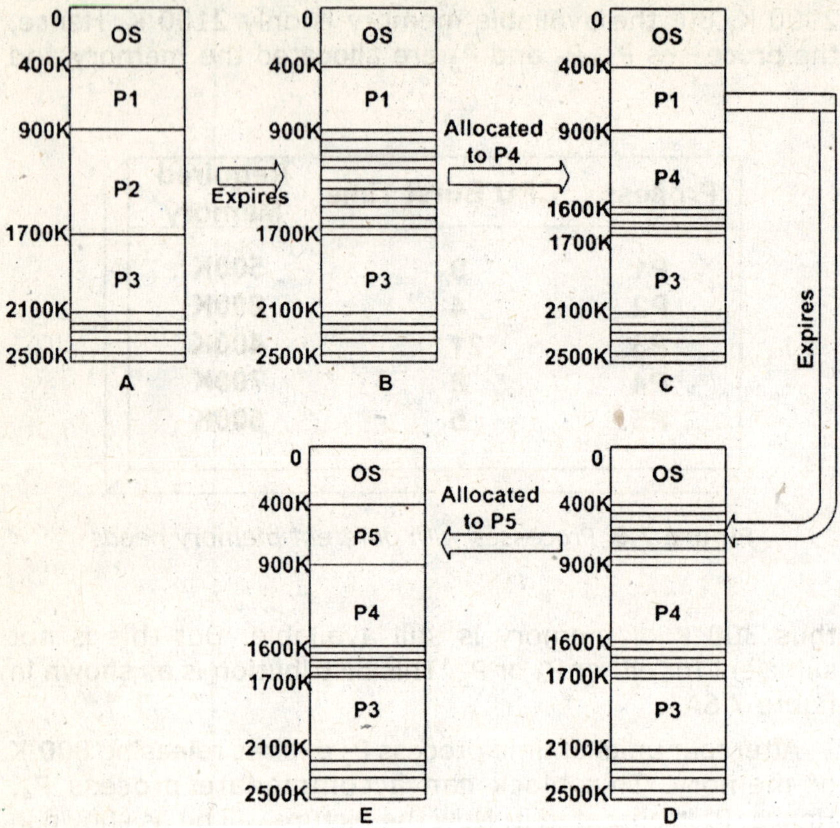

Figure 7.6 *Multiple partition allocation*

wasted memory. In the worst case, there could be a block of free memory between every pair of processes. Hence, in this sense, the multiple partition allocation algorithm is not much efficient.

There is another deficiency of this algorithm, which is known as internal fragmentation.

Consider a block of 7224 bytes. Suppose that a process requests 7221 bytes of memory. If we allocate exactly 7221 bytes we will be left with 3 bytes of memory. It is very difficult for the operating system to keep track of this small block. Hence, the entire block of 7224 bytes is allocated to that process, which results in the internal fragmentation of 3 bytes.

7.3.4 Compaction

A possible remedy to the problem of external fragmentation is compaction. The idea is to move all processes towards one end of memory and all the free blocks of memory towards the other end. For example, consider the case in which the blocks are distributed between 2 processes as shown in figure 7.7.

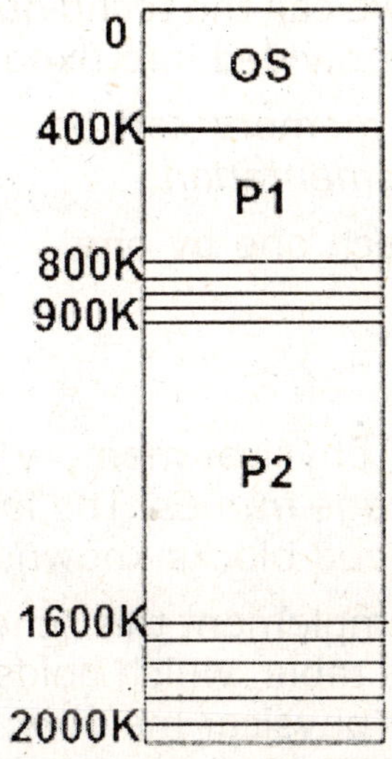

Figure 7.7 *Compaction*

Now, using the compaction algorithm, we move process P_2 upwards and the free block of 100 K between P_1 and P_2 downwards thus forming a big block of 500 K.

However, compaction is possible only when dynamic relocation is used i.e., when the address binding is done at run time.

7.4 Non-Contiguous Allocation

In the previous example we have made use of compaction because of the reason that the available memory is not contiguous. How will it be if a process could be split into two parts and each part is allocated a block of memory individually?

In the previous example, if a process requiring 500 K of memory is split into two sub processes, one process of 100 K and the other process of 400 K then, without making use of compaction, we can provide sufficient memory to that process.

This idea is the main background behind *non-contiguous* allocation.

If the chunks of memory have to be of same size for all the processes then we call the technique *paging*. In paging, the process image is divided into fixed sized pages.

If the chunks of memory can be of different sizes the method is called *segmentation*.

Now let us see each one by one.

7.4.1 Paging

In this scheme, the physical memory is divided into fixed sized blocks called *page frames*. The logical memory is also divided into equal sized blocks known as *pages*.

The hardware to implement this scheme, shown in figure 7.8, contains a page table, which holds the base addresses of each page in the physical memory. The logical address generated by the CPU is divided into two parts: a page number (p) and a page displacement (d). The page number is used as an index into the page table to get the base address. Now, the page displacement d and the base address b are combined to find out the physical address, which is then sent to the memory circuit.

Here a doubt may arise. The compiler generates only one-dimensional address in binary. How can it be split into two parts i.e., page number and page displacement? It is a doubt of worth. The secret here lies in the size of the page. If the page size is a power of 2, like 16, 32, 64 ... 1 K, 2 K etc. then the single binary address can be shown as a 2D address because some higher order bits automatically correspond to page number p and some lower order bits correspond to page displacement d. Hence, it is mandatory that the page size should be a power of 2.

With this paging scheme we can get rid of external fragmentation. However, there could be some internal

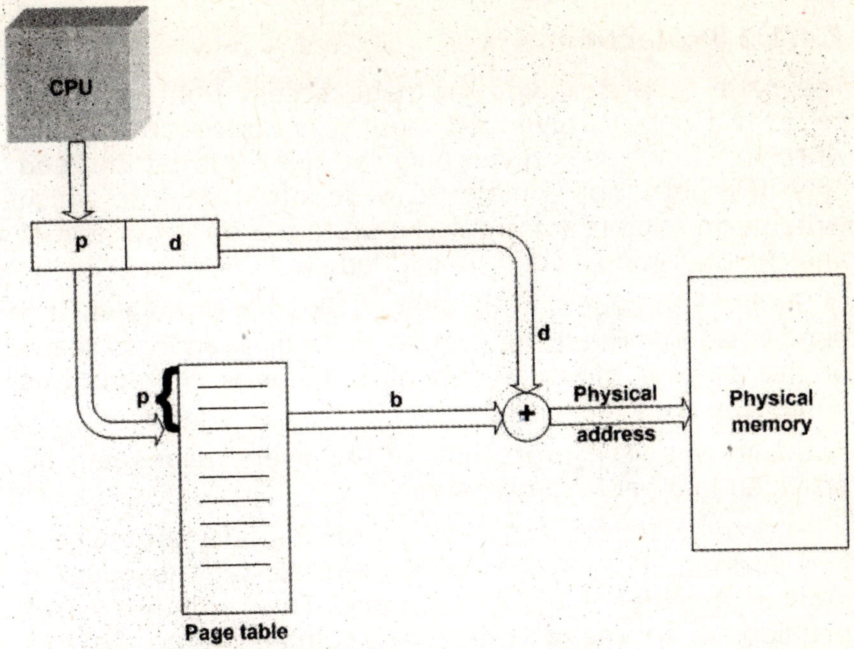

Figure 7.8 *Paging hardware*

fragmentation. Suppose that a process requires n pages of memory plus one byte. Since all the pages are of fixed size it will be allocated $n + 1$ pages and hence there is an internal fragmentation of almost a page.

This problem suggests that the page size should be as small as possible. However, a very small page size increases the overhead on the system to maintain the page table.

The scheme works as follows: When a process arrives and requests for memory, its requirement is measured in terms of pages. For example, if a process is of 32 Kb and the page size is 4 Kb then the process needs to be allocated 8 pages.

After this measurement, it is checked whether that many number of frames are available in the physical memory. If sufficient frames are available the process is allocated them. The first page of process is loaded into one of these frames and the frame number is noted in the page table of that process. Then the second page is loaded and the frame number is noted in the page table and so on.

7.4.1.1 Protection

The page table contains the page access rights to each page. If a page is given RW right it is both readable and writable. If a page is given only the right R it can be read only. If an attempt is made to write into a page to which write permission is not granted a system error is generated and the operating system is notified.

Similarly, a page can be defined as valid or invalid. If a page is set to valid it means that the logical address space of the process to which this page belongs contains this page otherwise it does not.

So, in this way, protection to the users' pages can be provided in a paged environment.

In systems that support a very large logical address space it is very laborious to maintain the page table because it alone consumes a lot of memory. The remedy to this problem is to use a two-level paging scheme. In this scheme, the page table is also paged.

For example, consider a system having a page size of 4 Kbytes. The logical address generated by the CPU is divided into a page number consisting of 20 bits and a page displacement of 12 bits. In two-level paging scheme, the page number is again divided into 10-bit page number and 10-bit displacement. This means, after two-level paging the logical address will be as shown in figure 7.9.

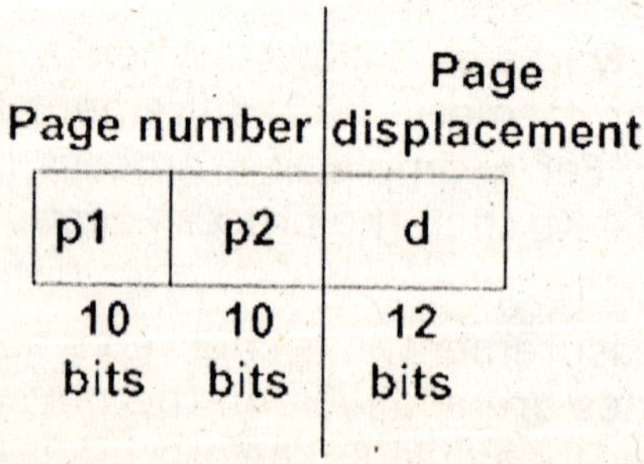

Figure 7.9 *Logical address after 2-level paging*

Here, P_1 acts as an index into the outer page table and P_2 is the page displacement (within the outer page table).

Similar to two-level paging there are three-level and four-level paging schemes also.

Although the number of memory accesses to convert the logical address into physical address increases with multilevel paging the performance of the system remains reasonable.

Since maintaining page tables, whose purpose is just to maintain a record of how other physical memory is being used, consumes a lot of memory, we can use an inverted page table as a remedy to this problem. Each entry in the inverted page table is a pair of process id and page number. And the logical address generated by the CPU contains process id, page number and page displacement.

During a memory reference the inverted page table is searched using process id and page number. If a process with these details is found then its displacement in the inverted page table and the actual page displacement in the logical address generated by the CPU are added to generate the physical address. If a match is not found a system error is generated.

The main drawback of this scheme is the amount of time needed to search the table is more. This problem can be, to some extent, eliminated using hash tables.

The main advantage of paging scheme is the possibility to share the common code. That means, only one copy of the code will be in the memory, which can be accessed simultaneously by different users. The constraint for the code to be shared is that it should be reentrant. That means it should not be changed during execution. All the users will be issued read permission only.

7.4.2 Segmentation

The main difference between paging and segmentation is that pages are physical in nature and hence fixed in size, whereas segments are logical divisions of a program and hence, in general, they are of variable size.

There are code segment, data segment and stack segment in every program in its executable form. Moreover, each segment may have further segments in it. For example, in a program we will be using several prewritten and precompiled functions like *sqrt*, *sin*, *cos* etc. All these functions can be considered as separate segments.

For example, consider a program having the following segments.

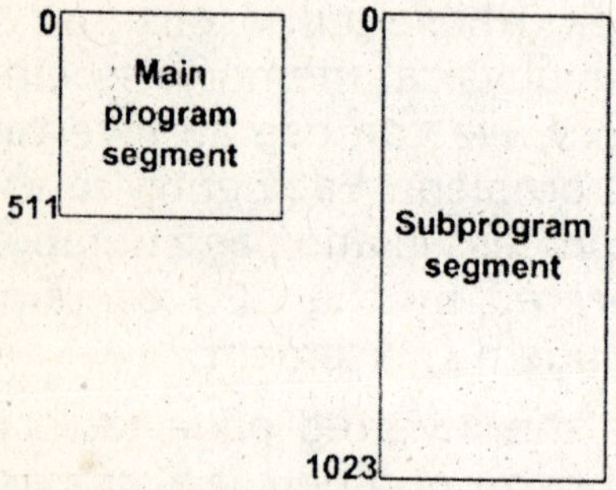

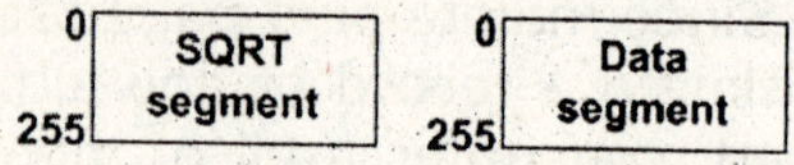

Segment Number	Size
0	512
1	1024
2	256
3	256
Total	2048

Figure 7.10 *Different segments of a program*

As shown in figure 7.10, each segment is compiled with respect to 0 as the starting address for that segment.

In connection with segmentation, it is the duty of the compiler or linkage editor to recognize different segments, number them, build the segment table and finally produce an executable image by assigning two-dimensional addresses.

In segmentation, the address consists of segment number and a displacement within that segment. Here, the segment size is unpredictable. Hence, the address should be specified explicitly in 2D form.

The page table influences the mapping from 2D, user-defined address into one-dimensional address. Each entry in the segment table consists of two parts: the starting address or the segment base and segment limit. The segment number s is used as an index into the segment table. The displacement *d* must be between 0 and segment limit. If the offset or displacement is legal, it is added to the starting address or segment base to produce the physical address.

We use segment table base register and length register also when the number of segments is large.

Similar to paging scheme, segmentation also has some type of protective measures to prevent illegal accesses to data or programs. Each segment table entry is associated with some protection bits, which are checked by the memory-mapping network whenever a memory reference occurs.

Also, the segmentation scheme allows common sharing of code in a similar fashion as paging. Sharing is said to be done when entries in the segment table of two different processes point to the same physical memory locations.

Although segmentation results in external fragmentation, it can be avoided with compaction. Since, by nature, segmentation is dynamic relocation algorithm, compaction can easily be done. Another approach to counteract the external fragmentation problem is to maintain small segments.

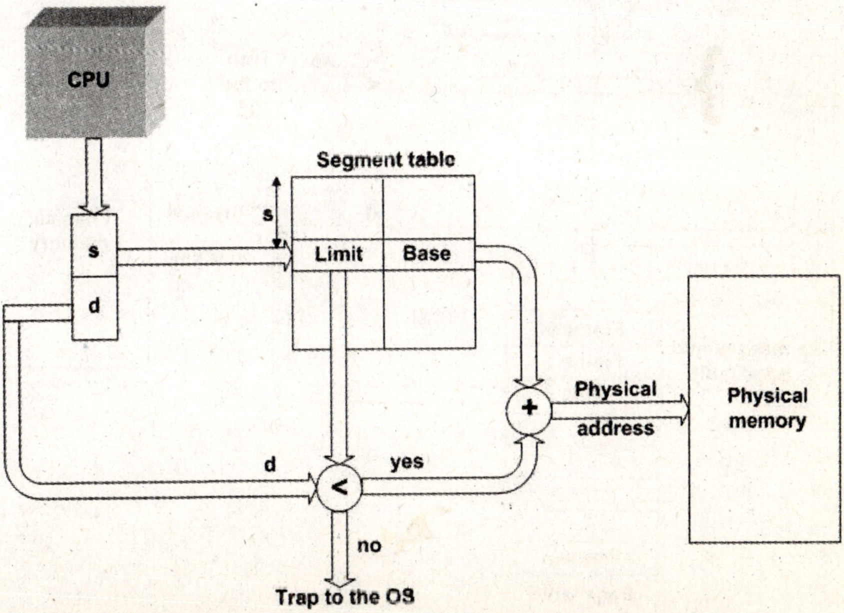

Figure 7.11 *Hardware to implement segmentation*

7.4.3 Segmentation with Paging

Both segmentation and paging have their advantages and disadvantages.

With segments of large size, say 64 Kwords, the average segment size and external fragmentation may pose some problems in segmentation. Moreover, the average search time to locate a segment will also be large.

Hence, a different approach is adopted to solve this problem, which is to *page* the *segments*.

In segmentation with paging, the virtual address has three parts - segment number (*s*), page number within that

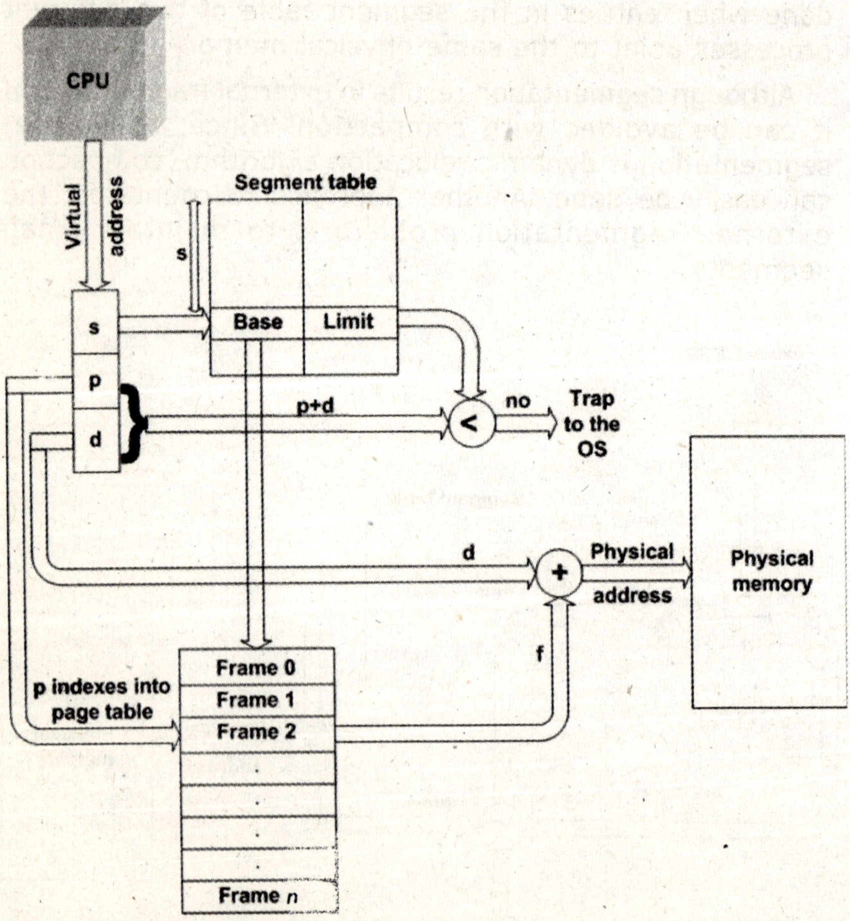

Figure 7.12 *Paged segmentation hardware*

segment (*p*) and offset within the page (*d*). A segment table entry is the base address of the page table for a particular segment rather than that of the segment itself. The segment number is used as an index into the segment table to find out the base address of the page table for that segment. The page number indexes into the page table to find out the frame number. Then the frame number and page offset are added to obtain the physical address.

This is illustrated in figure 7.12.

Review Questions

1. What are various memory management schemes?
2. Explain the key issues of memory management.
3. Differentiate between logical address and physical address.
4. What is the significance of swapping?
5. Explain single partition scheme of memory allocation.
6. Explain the problem of internal fragmentation in single partition allocation scheme.
7. Explain how the problem of internal fragmentation is eliminated in multiple partition allocation scheme?
8. How compaction eliminates the problem of external fragmentation?
9. Explain the concept of paging.
10. Explain how the memory is protected in paging.
11. What is the main difference between paging and segmentation?
12. Can the two concepts - segmentation and paging be implemented together? Explain.

CHAPTER

8

Virtual Memory

Introduction

This chapter talks about a different memory management scheme that helps the operating system serve more number of processes than what it could using ordinary memory management schemes.

8.1 Virtual Memory

The main requirement of all the memory management schemes we have covered in the previous chapter is that the entire process must be in main memory before it can execute. But the physical memory is always limited and hence the number of processes that can be accommodated in the main memory and hence the degree of multiprogramming is less. Also, during swapping, the entire process image needs to be swapped out.

Now, virtual memory is a concept that allows a process to start executing with only a part of it loaded into the main memory.

It has been shown experimentally that the entire program is not needed in many cases. Even if the entire program is needed it may not **all** be needed at the same time. This forms the background for *virtual memory* systems.

The main advantage of virtual memory is that we can maintain a large virtual memory. That means a program will never be constrained by the amount of physical memory available. Another advantage is that the speed of each process increases to a considerable extent.

8.2 Demand Paging

In general, demand paging is used to implement virtual memory. In demand paging, the *pager* plays a crucial role. It swaps in only those pages of a process which are necessary at that moment. The remaining pages remain on the disk.

Demand paging works as follows:

Every process starts with some pages in memory. During execution, if an instruction is encountered that refers to any instruction or data in some other page, which is not present in the main memory, a page fault occurs. Then the operating system brings that required page into main memory and restarts the process. In this way, all the desired pages for a process are brought into the memory *on demand*. In the extreme case, a process can start executing without even a single page in the memory.

All the pages of a process that are not in the main memory are stored on a backing store, which is generally a fast disk. The pager swaps the essential pages into the memory. An interesting question here is how and when to tell the pager to swap in a particular page?

The simplest possible way to do this is to use a *valid - invalid* bit scheme. We may use the valid bit to indicate that a page is legal and is in memory. And, the invalid bit is used to indicate that that page is currently on the disk. When the process tries to access this page, a page fault occurs. And the operating system is notified through a trap generated by paging hardware that an attempt is made to access a page that is not available in the memory. Then the operating system brings the desired page into the memory and thus the path is made clear for the process to continue.

Now, consider a special case. Suppose that there are 20 frames available in the physical memory and that there are three 10-page processes each of which needs only 5 out of the 10 pages to start with. In this way, after loading all these processes into memory 5 more frames will be free. So we can allocate these 5 also to another process. Now, here is an interesting question. What happens if each of these processes wants to access all of its 10 pages suddenly? In response to the page faults generated by these processes the operating system tries to read the desired pages into memory. But it finds that there are no frames available. So what should the operating system do in this context? It has only two possibilities:

- To terminate the user process
- To replace a page

The first method is inefficient because it lowers the degree of multiprogramming and hence the CPU utilization. Also, the throughput decreases. Hence, the operating system has to opt for page replacement.

8.3 Page Replacement

The page replacement scheme works as follows:

At first a page frame that is not currently in active use is detected and is made free by writing its contents into swap space. Now, the desired page is loaded into this new free frame. Later, the page table is modified as required.

Thus, if we succeed in providing a solution to overcome the hurdles just mentioned we could enjoy the benefits offered by the concept of demand paging. And the solution is to implement page replacement. There are several algorithms to achieve this. Some of them are:

- Optimal (OPT)
- First in first out (FIFO)
- Second chance (SC)
- Not recently used (NRU)
- Least recently used (LRU)

- LRU approximation
- Not frequency used

Let us study these algorithms one by one.

8.3.1 Optimal (OPT) Algorithm

Its theme is to replace the page that will not be used immediately in the near future. Because the practical implementation of this algorithm requires future knowledge about a page this is not widely used. However, this algorithm guarantees the lowest possible page fault rate for a specific number of frames.

Now consider the following page reference string

4 1 3 2 8 3 5 1 6 8 4 8

This is the sequence in which the logical pages are referenced in a program during its execution. Assume that there are only 3 page frames 0, 1, 2 and that all of them are initially empty.

Now observe the table in figure 8.1.

Page reference sequence	4	1	3	2	8	3	5	1	6	8	4	8
Frame 0	4	4	4	2	8	8	8	8	8	8	8	8
Frame 1		1	1	1	1	1	1	1	6	6	6	6
Frame 2			3	3	3	3	5	5	5	5	4	4

Figure 8.1 *Optimal algorithm*

Initially, page 4 is loaded into frame 0, then page 1 into frame 1, and then page 3 into frame 2. Now, to load page 2 there is no free frame. Hence, a page fault occurs as described in one of the previous sections. In response to this page fault, the operating system checks the sequence for the page that is not needed in the near future. This approach directs the operating system to replace page 4. Similarly, in the next reference page 2 is replaced by 8 and during next page fault page 3 is replaced by page 5. And this process continues until the end of the sequence is reached.

This is undoubtedly the best algorithm. But, as said earlier, it is very difficult to know future references well in advance. Hence, this algorithm is confined to theoretical purposes and analyses.

8.3.2 First In First Out (FIFO) Algorithm

The working of this algorithm is simple. The page that is loaded into memory first is removed first. For example, consider the same sequence as before.

4 1 3 2 8 3 5 1 6 8 4 8

Now observe figure 8.2.

Page reference sequence	4	1	3	2	8	3	5	1	6	8	4	8
Frame 0	4	4	4	2	2	2	2	1	1	1	4	4
Frame 1		1	1	1	8	8	8	8	6	6	6	6
Frame 2			3	3	3	3	5	5	5	8	8	8

Figure 8.2 *FIFO algorithm*

The first 3 columns require no explanation. From the 4th column we can observe that to load page 2, page 4 is removed since it entered the memory first. Similarly, to load page 8, page 1 is removed and a similar approach continues through out.

This algorithm is very simple to understand and implement.

8.3.3 Second Chance (SC) Algorithm

This algorithm replaces the pages that are not referenced quite often. In this scheme, each page is given a reference bit. If the page is referenced its reference bit will be 1 otherwise, it will be 0.

This algorithm is essentially a FIFO algorithm. When a page is selected its reference bit is checked. If it is 0, the operating system proceeds to replace this page. If it is 1, that page is given a *second chance* and is not replaced until all the other pages are given a second chance. In this way, this algorithm works.

8.3.4 Not Recently Used (NRU) Algorithm

Before replacing a page, this algorithm checks -

- Whether the page is referenced or not
- Whether the page is modified or not

The 2 bits attached to each page frame answer the above 2 questions. The convention is as shown in figure 8.3.

Class	Reference bit	Modification bit	Description
A	0	0	Not referenced, not modified
B	0	1	Not referenced, modified
C	1	0	Referenced, not modified
D	1	1	Referenced, modified

Figure 8.3 *Conventions for NRU*

Class A pages are replaced first, and then class B pages and so on.

8.3.5 Least Recently Used (LRU) Algorithm

This algorithm can be considered as an approximation to the optimal algorithm. It attaches with each page the time it is last referenced. The page that has not been used for the longest period is replaced first when the necessity comes. Unlike the optimal algorithm here we need to look backward.

As an example, consider the same sequence we studied in the previous algorithms:

4 1 3 2 8 3 5 1 6 8 4 8

Now observe figure 8.4.

Page reference sequence	4	1	3	2	8	3	5	1	6	8	4	8
Frame 0	4	4	4	2	2	2	5	5	5	8	8	8
Frame 1		1	1	1	8	8	8	1	1	1	4	4
Frame 2			3	3	3	3	3	3	6	6	6	6

Figure 8.4 *LRU algorithm*

Observe the fourth column. To load page 2, page 4 is removed, because among the pages 4, 1, 3, page 4 is least recently used. Similarly, to load page 8, page 1 is replaced. The same approach continues through out.

This is the best algorithm, which resembles the optimal algorithm in many aspects. However, it is very costly and difficult to implement.

There are 2 famous methods to implement this algorithm: *stack*, and *counters*.

- *Stack:*

  The LRU algorithm can be implemented using a double linked list. When a page is referenced it is removed from its current position and placed on the top of the stack. Thus the top of the stack always contains the page that is most recently used and the bottom of the stack contains the process that is least recently used. So when it becomes necessary to replace a page the page at the bottom of the stack is removed.

- *Counters:*

  This method requires 2 long registers, one to attach to the CPU, which functions as a clock and the other to attach to each page frame.

  Whenever a memory reference occurs the clock is incremented. The contents of the clock register are copied into the register associated with that page frame. Thus we can know the time of the last reference of each page. The page with smallest time value is replaced on demand.

Now, here is an interesting question. If the amount of free memory is fixed how can we distribute it among several processes? The answer is that the distribution is done with the help of some algorithms like *equal allocation* and *proportional allocation*.

- *Equal allocation:*

  If, for example, consider that there is 122 K of free memory available and that 3 processes are competing for it. Then this available memory is divided by the number of processes, 3 in this case. Thus, each process will be allocated 122 / 3 = 40 K and the remaining 2 K will be stored for future use.

- *Proportional allocation:*

  Equal allocation yields best results when used in the case of processes comparable in size. For example, if one process is of 150 K and the other process is of 10 K and these are the only processes competing then it is not wise to distribute the available memory equally between these 2 processes. Here we have to use proportional allocation algorithm, which distributes the available memory among processes depending on their size. Thus a process of larger size gets more number of frames.

8.4 Thrashing

Let us now discuss another interesting topic. Suppose that a process is allocated *n* frames and that all these frames are in active use. If the process wants to reference another new page it will have to page fault and replace a page, which it will need again shortly. Consequently, it will page fault again very quickly. Thus the page faults occur very frequently (one after another) and the process spends much of its time paging than executing. This peculiar situation is known as **thrashing**.

Whenever the CPU observes its utilization to be low, it increases the degree of multiprogramming by introducing some more new processes into the system. As the number of frames is limited, eventually these newly entered processes may need to page fault. Thus a queue will be formed for the paging device and hence the CPU utilization decreases. So the CPU scheduler again increases the degree of multiprogramming. Again these processes have to compete for frames and hence they also enter the queue for paging device. Thus the CPU utilization further decreases and hence the CPU scheduler again brings in some more new processes, which also enter the queue for the paging device. In this way, the page fault rage increases tremendously and no work will be done and thrashing is said to occur.

Thrashing can be prevented by allocating all the frames a process needs. We can use the *working set* strategy to know how many frames a process needs.

The working set scheme makes use of a parameter *d* to define the working set. If a page falls in the most recent *d* references it is considered to be the working set i.e., a page in active use lies in the working set and a page, which is no longer used, drops from the working set. The efficiency of this strategy depends upon the value of *d*. Hence, we need to choose *d* so cautiously.

The operating system observes the working set of each process and allocates it as many frames as it needs depending upon its size. If still some frames are left another process is started. When the sum of the working set sizes of different processes increases the operating system chooses a process to suspend. All the frames allocated to that process are freed and reallocated to another new process. When the frames are available the suspended process can be restarted if it succeeds in the competition.

Thus, the working set strategy prevents thrashing and increases CPU utilization. However, there is a small difficulty with this scheme, which is to keep track of the working set. This tracking can be maintained with the help of a reference bit and a fixed-interval timer interrupt.

There is yet another scheme to prevent the problem of thrashing, which works by studying the page fault frequency.

If the page fault rate of a process is high it indicates that the process needs more pages. On the other hand, if it is low then the process is having excess number of frames. This scheme defines an upper limit and a lower limit. If the page fault rate crosses this upper limit then that process is allocated another frame. If the page fault rate falls below the lower limit a frame is removed from that process. In this way thrashing can be prevented.

Some more important considerations in a paging system are:

- *Prepaging:*

  When a swapped out process, which has all its pages on the disk, is to be restarted each of its pages needs to be brought into the memory. The same could be the scene each time this process is to be swapped in (if it happens to be swapped out of memory more than once). Now, prepaging is a strategy that brings in, at one time, all the pages that will be needed by the process.

- *Page size:*

  There is no universally accepted idea about the page size. Although a smaller page size offers some benefits like accurate matching of program locality, better utilization of memory it is very difficult to compensate for the loss generated due to the very large increase in the number of page faults. Hence, the trend now-a-days is towards a larger page size.

- *Demand segmentation:*

  In this scheme, the memory is maintained in segments rather than pages. The operating system keeps track of these segments with the help of segment descriptors. Similar to demand paging, here also a process does not need to have all its segments in the main memory to execute. A process starts executing with some predetermined number of segments. When a process addresses a segment, which is in main memory, the execution continues unhindered. If that segment is not in the memory the operating system swaps out a segment and brings in the requested segment.

The segment replacement is carried out by noting the *accessed bit* in the segment descriptor. With the help of this bit the operating system can know which segment is to be replaced. Although demand segmentation can be implemented with the aid of less sophisticated hardware it requires more overhead. Hence, this scheme is not generally used to provide virtual memory.

Review Questions

1. What is the advantage of virtual memory?
2. Explain the concept of demand paging in detail.
3. What is the necessity of page replacement?
4. Explain different page replacement algorithms in detail.
5. Explain the least recently used algorithm with an example.
6. What is thrashing?

CHAPTER 9

The Concept of Files

Introduction

'Today the server is down. It has taken a long time even for a text *file* to download'. 'Bitmap *files* consume a lot of memory. You better go for JPG or GIF'. 'Our hard disk capacity is so large that we have dumped more than 5 movie *files* into it' - File: the most common term we come across everyday. This chapter, which starts with the definition of a file, explains various concepts related to file systems present in currently available operating systems.

9.1 What is a File?

In simple terms, a file can be defined as a *collection of logical records that consist of related information*. This collection is assigned a name by the operating system. Here the point to be talked about is why and when do we need to define a file?

Suppose that you are creating a text file using 'MS Word'. You have typed a few pages and decided to continue your work sometime later. Then you would need to do something before coming out of that program (MS Word in this case). Yes, you need to save the matter you have typed.

If you are using MS Windows, a dialog box titled '*save as*' would appear when you have opted for saving the typed information, which asks you to give a name to that piece of 'related information'.

When you type in a name and click on '*ok*' button the dialog box disappears and that information, which is text in this case, will be saved as a '*file*' with the name you have given to it, on the secondary storage device like a disk.

Afterwards, if you want to edit the file you can do it by opening it in write mode.

Thus we need to define a file when it becomes necessary to store logically related data as a collection on a secondary storage device. It can be said in a more general sense like this: if some data is available on the disk or any secondary storage device it is available in the form of files. Depending upon the type of that data the files can be of several types like *text* files, *executable* files, *object* files, *image* files etc.

Here a doubt may arise - we are just specifying the name of the file but how does the operating system distinguish between various types of files? The technique most commonly used to achieve such an implementation is to divide the file name into two parts: file's actual name and extension. Usually a period (dot) separates the file name and the extension. Here the file name is used to identify the name of the file and extension is used to identify the type of the file.

For example, a text file created using Windows notepad it will be saved with a *.txt* extension indicating that it is a text file. Similarly, *.exe* extension implies that the file name is an executable one. The table in figure 9.1 gives you an idea of various file types and their extensions.

9.2 File Attributes

'Name' is certainly the first and very important attribute of any file, which is used to identify a particular file from a collection of many. The attributes of a file give the information about it. Although these attributes vary from

File type	Extension
Text	text, doc
Source code	a, asm, p, f77
Batch	bat, sh
Library	lib, a
Object	obj, o
Executable	exe, com

Figure 9.1 *Various file types*

one operating system to another, there are certain common attributes about which a small description is given below.

- *Name:* As it has been said earlier, the file name is a very essential attribute that can be set by the creator of the file. It is possible to change the name of the file in future, with the extension remaining the same.
- *Size:* This attribute gives an idea about how much space did the file consume. Text files consume a very small memory when compared to multimedia files, which require several megabytes of memory. The size of a file plays a vital role in transferring the file from one location to the other, for example, copying the file from the hard disk to the floppy disk or transferring the file from one computer to another computer through FTP.
- *Location:* This attribute tells us where the file resides in the memory. For the convenience of the user the available secondary memory is divided into different partitions.
- *Date:* This attribute gives very useful information about the date when the file is created, when it is last modified etc.

Apart from these common attributes there can be several other attributes giving further important information about the FAPs (File-Access-Permissions). depending upon the operating system.

9.3 Operations on Files

A file is said to be defined 'completely' when all the operations that can be performed on it are specified. In general, there are six basic operations that can be performed on *any* file. The operating system generates different system calls to perform these operations. Below is small description about each of these 6 operations.

- *Creating a file:* A file is created after sufficient space for it is found on the file system. After the file is created, an entry into the directory for this newly created file is made.
- *Writing to a file:* This is accomplished with the help of a write pointer. At first, a system call is made with the name of the file as the chief parameter. Then the entire directory is searched for that file and the location of the file is found. Now, it is yet another duty of the operating system to maintain a write pointer with the file, the duty of which is to point to the location where the next write is to take place.
- *Reading from a file:* Here also a system call is made to search for the file to be read with its name as the parameter. Similar to the previous case, here also, the entire directory is searched for the file and the location where the file currently resides is found out. The operating system maintains a read pointer in this case, the duty of which is to point to the location within the file where from the next read is to take place.
- *Repositioning within a file:* In this case also, the first step is common, which is to search for the file in the directory. Repositioning, since takes place within a file, does not require any I/O to be performed.
- *Truncating a file:* This function allows the user to keep all the attributes of the file unchanged (of course, the length would change) while erasing out its contents. This way, the user does not need to delete the file and then recreate it.

- *Deleting a file:* It is opposite to that of creating a file, in effect. At first, the directory is searched for the file and if it is found all the space allocated to it is freed and then its entry from the directory is removed. This freed space can be used for other purposes.

Using these basic operations several other desired operations like copying a file into a floppy disk or a printer etc. can be performed.

In this way, we make use of certain operations to store some information in a file in the required format. This information from the files may be accessed either by 'sequential access method' or by 'direct access method'. The sequential access method is based on the tape model of a file in which the information in the file is processed in a sequential order. On the other hand, the direct access method is based on the disk model of a file. In this method, a file is made up of certain fixed length logical records. Any of these blocks can be accessed without following a specific order. That means these blocks can be accessed randomly.

9.4 The Concept of Directories

Suppose that your computer system consists of several hundreds of files. To manage all these data is undoubtedly a cumbersome process and hence it becomes necessary to organize them. Making use of the concept of directories is a very good and efficient way to organize such a huge structure. The directory records all the information such as name, location, size and type about the files in it. If the capacity of the hard disk is very large then, in such cases, the disk is divided into several partitions, each containing separate root directories.

As it has been said earlier, a directory contains the information about the files in it. Now, to further enhance the ease in managing those files, the directory itself can be organized in several different ways by performing some operations on it. Below is a brief description about the basic operations that can be performed on a typical directory structure.

- *List a directory:* We want to list all the files in a directory and the details of each file.
- *Create/delete a file:* Within a directory new files may be created and if a file is no longer needed it may be deleted from the directory.
- *Search for a file:* Given the name of a file, we should be able to search the entire directory structure to find it out.
- *Rename a file:* We may want to change the name of a file in order to make it more convenient to identify its contents.

In what follows, appears a detailed study about the schemes to define the logical structure of a directory.

9.4.1 Single Level Directory

It is the simplest possible directory structure. All the files in the system are contained in a single directory. The main problem in this type of directory structure is the difficulty that arises when the number of files in the system increases. Since the names of all files need to be different the overhead to choose different names increases with increase in the number of files.

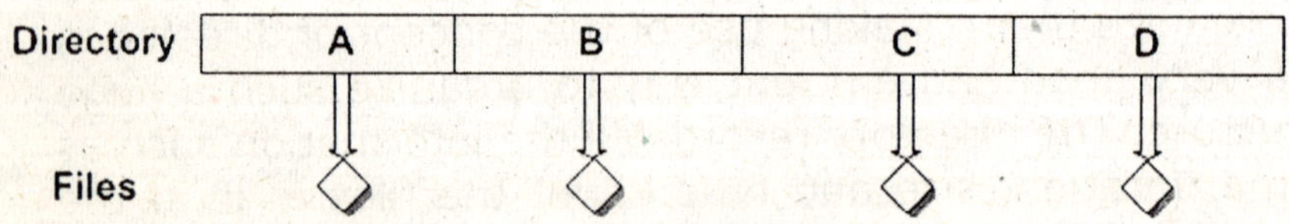

Figure 9.2 *Single level directory*

9.4.2 Two Level Directory

When the number of users increases the organization becomes very difficult with the single level directory structure. Hence, we go for the two level directory structure, in which every user can have a directory of his own.

In two level directory structure the problem of choosing

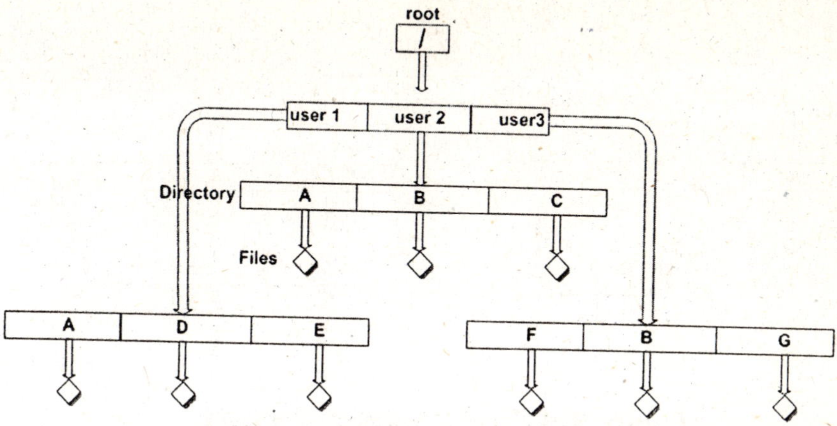

Figure 9.3 *Two level directory*

different names will not be as severe as in the case of a single level directory because the same name may be assigned to different files in different directories.

The users may have access to the files in the directories of other users. However, the procedure to access the files varies from one operating system to another.

9.4.3 Tree Structured Directories

Tree structured directory is a generalization of two-level directory with an arbitrary height. Each user has his own directory and he can organize his files creating further more new directories known as sub-directories. The path name for every file in the system is unique. The path name of a file is the path from the root to all sub-directories to the specified file.

The directory in which the user is currently working is known as *present working directory* (PWD). All the files the user may want to access typically lie in his PWD. But sometimes the user may want to access a file, which is not in his PWD. Then he needs to specify the entire path name of that file or simply he may change to the directory in which the file resides by performing the required system call, say *change directory*. [Check this procedure with windows operating system in which we search for the file

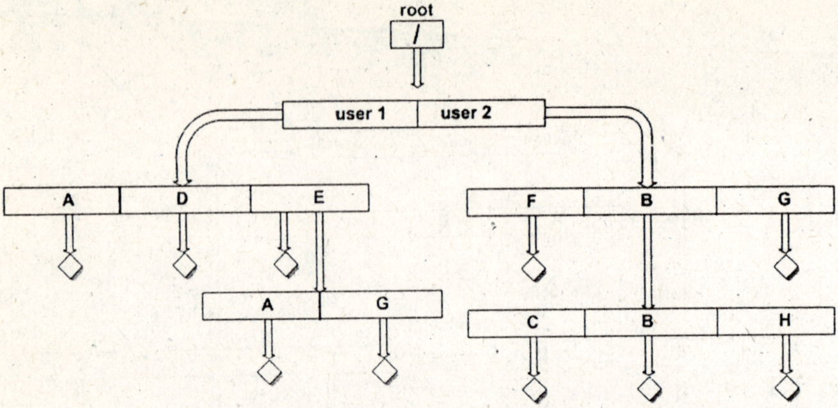

Figure 9.4 *Tree structured directory*

of interest by selecting the 'Search' option from the 'Start' menu. We specify the directory where the file probably lies (or we may opt for searching all the drives C, D, A etc.) If the file is found its name along with its details (location, size, date last modified etc.) would be displayed and we may access that file by just double-clicking it.]

9.4.4 Acyclic-graph Directories

In the tree structured directory method of organizing the files, there is a restraint to *share* files or directories.

The Acyclic-graph directory structure allows the files or directories to be shared by different users. For example, consider the case where several project members want to access the same files. Then, in general, all these files are put in a directory, which is made accessible to all the members.

A user who wants to access a particular file in this shared directory may do so by opening the link that exists in his directory, which is a pointer to that file. In this way, the links to all the shared files appear in the directories of all the users. Here the point to be noted is that the changes made by a user in a file appear to all the users because every user will be accessing the same file but not its copy. Although there is another method to implement the shared files concept, which is to make the copies of the *shared directory*

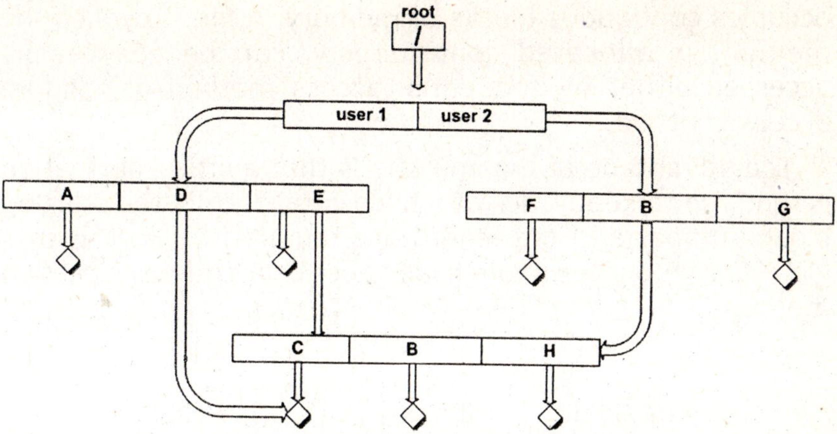

Figure 9.5 *Acyclic graph directory*

available in all the user directories, the implementation using links is preferred because of the facility offered by it when the necessity to delete a shared file or to find out the path name comes.

So far, we discussed the mainly used methods to implement the directory structures. Because of the problems involved with the acyclic graph structures, tree directory structures are used more commonly.

Thus, this is a study about the file system interface. This file system is stored permanently on the secondary storage, typically a disk. In the next section, we study various methods to allocate space to the files.

9.5 Allocation Methods

The files are allocated space through one of the three methods listed below:

- Contiguous allocation
- Linked allocation
- Indexed allocation

9.5.1 Contiguous Allocation

We have studied earlier that the entire available disk space is divided into a set of blocks. In contiguous allocation, a file occupies contiguous blocks of memory. A file, to which the memory is allocated contiguously, can be very easily accessed either by sequential access method or random access method.

The advantage of this method is that a little information is required to keep track of a file's details. Only the starting block number and the length are required to work with a file. Figure 9.6 gives a rough idea about contiguous allocation method.

File Name	Starting block number	Length
Notes.txt	2	10
Tree.bmp	60	49
Book.doc	420	600

Figure 9.6 *Contiguous allocation*

The major problem with contiguous allocation is external fragmentation. Although compaction can eliminate this problem, the time taken for compacting the available free blocks of memory is very high.

The other problem with this algorithm is determining how much space a file needs. It is very difficult to estimate, before the file is created, the memory requirement of it.

Whatever may be the algorithm we use it is almost impossible to allocate exactly the same amount of memory required by a file. The space assigned will be either more or less than what is actually required by the file. If the memory allocated is not sufficient for a file the user program is terminated mentioning the inadequacy of memory. To avoid this problem a file is always allocated more memory than what it requires. And, this trade-off sometimes leads to internal fragmentation, of course.

9.5.2 Linked Allocation

This algorithm solves the problems associated with

contiguous allocation. Linked allocation maintains the file as a linked list of memory blocks, which need not be contiguous. The file starts at a particular location in the memory and ends somewhere else. The directory contains a pointer to the first and last blocks of the file. Since any free block can be assigned to a file, the problem of external fragmentation does not arise with linked allocation.

However, linked allocation also offers a problem. This method can be used only with sequential access. It does not work effectively with random access.

The pointers also pose some problems. A considerable percentage of memory will be utilized only by these pointers. Also, if a particular pointer is lost because of some problems in the system and if the operating system picks up a wrong pointer many errors are likely to occur.

However, these problems are not very serious and can be solved by taking some precautionary measures like collecting the memory blocks into clusters. Figure 9.7 illustrates linked allocation method.

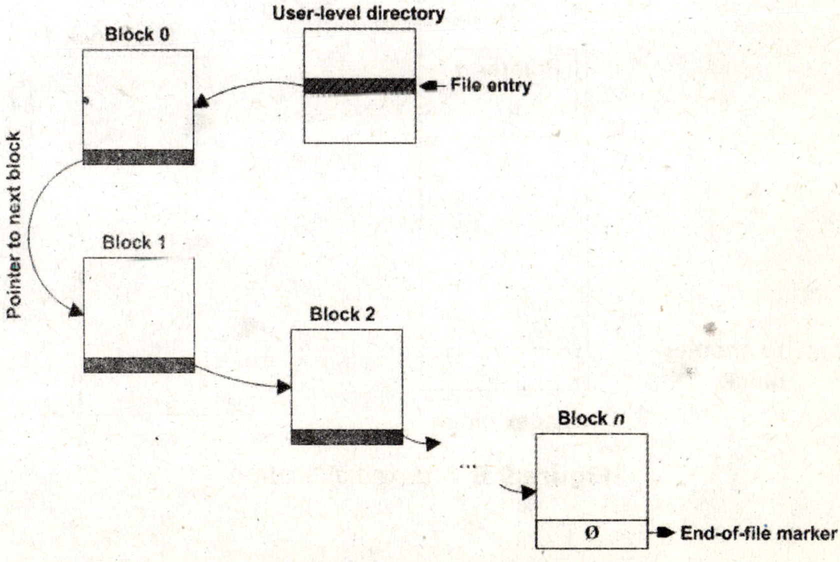

Figure 9.7 *Linked allocation*

9.5.3 Indexed Allocation

In indexed allocation, all the pointers are brought together into one block known as the index block.

Each file contains an index block of its own, which maintains all the addresses of its disk blocks. The main block of the directory, in which a file is present, contains the address of the file's index block.

Indexed allocation supports direct or random allocation. However, indexed allocation is more complex than the previous two allocation algorithms. Figure 9.8 illustrates indexed allocation.

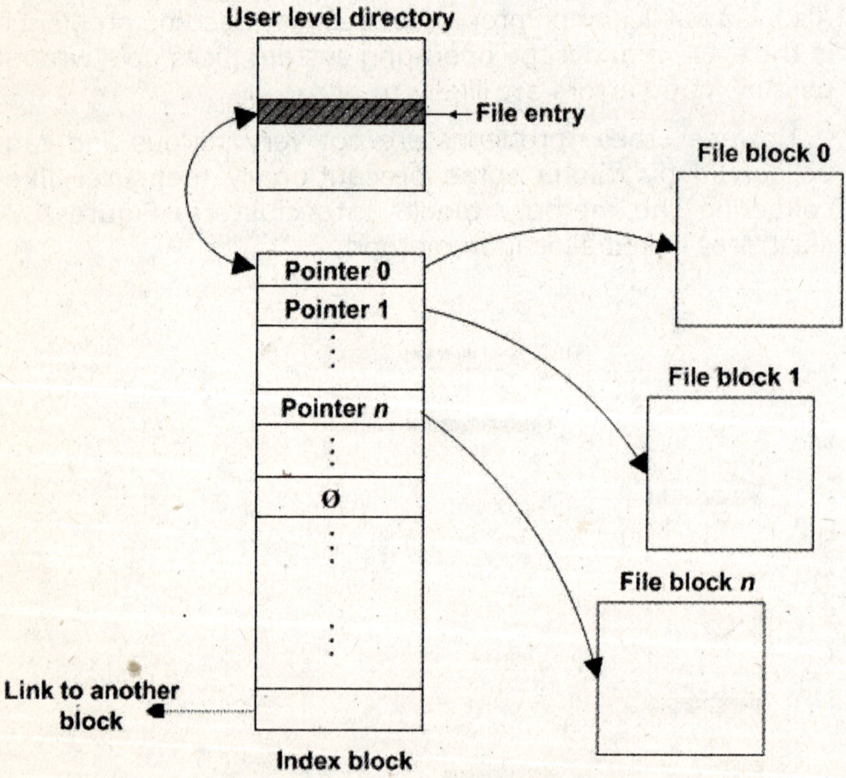

Figure 9.8 *Indexed allocation*

Review Questions

1. What are the different file extensions?
2. What are the different types of files?
3. What are the different attributes of files?
4. What operations can be performed on files?
5. What is the significance of directories?
6. What are the different directory structures?
7. In how many ways can a file be allocated space?
8. What is the drawback of contiguous allocation?

CHAPTER

10

Security and Protection

Introduction

Security is concerned with the ability of the operating system to enforce control over the storage and transportation of data in and among the objects such as files that the operating system supports.

A system is said to be secure when the information stored in it and in its physical resources is protected from unauthorized access, intentional alteration and accidental introduction of inconsistency.

10.1 Threats to Security

The threats of security in any computing environment can be classified into 2 categories: *active* threats and *passive* threats.

Active threats are again of 3 types:

- Unauthorized alteration or deletion of information (*amendments*)
- Unauthorized fabrication of information (*fabrication*)
- Denial of service to authorized users (*denial*)

Passive threats are of 2 types:

- Unauthorized use of service (*tapping*)
- Unauthorized disclosure of information (*disclosure*)

Security threats can arise as a result of deliberate or unintentional activities to utilize or access data. Unfortunately, it is not possible to achieve a 100% secure system. However, the cost for penetration can be made sufficiently large so that malicious attempts to penetrate are deterred.

10.2 Attacks on Security

- *Authentication:* Generally, to authenticate a user identity, user passwords are used. Attacks can be made on the system's security in this regard in some of the following ways:
  - ¤ The password of an authentic user is stolen and then is used by an intruder.
  - ¤ The intruder may try to find out the password by trail and error method.
  - ¤ The intruder may modify the password when an authentic user logs on to a system and temporarily goes away from it.
- *Line tapping:* Making use of some different and specially designed hardware and techniques, the intruder may try to tap the communication lines and access or even modify the data.
- *Browsing:* In many systems, the system files have permissive file access controls. In such cases, the intruder can browse through the system files and get the information about the access controls to different files in the system. Once he gets that information his job of accessing unprotected files or databases becomes very easy.
- *Rogue software:* Sometimes, the intruder may write a special program, which is intended to cause damage

to the data in the system. 'Virus' is a very famous type of such programs. Virus programming requires a deep knowledge of the operating system and the hardware.

- *Waste recovery:* Sometimes one or more blocks deleted from a file may contain different passwords. Though a block is deleted from a file and added to the list of free blocks, its contents remain unaltered until it is allocated to some other file and data is written into it. The intruder may somehow get access to such free blocks and know the passwords.

10.3 System Threats

10.3.1 Computer Worms

A computer worm is a full-fledged program written in such a way that it spreads to other computers over a network consuming the network resources to a large extent. It has the potential to bring the entire network to a halt.

A computer worm operates usually on a network. Each node on the network maintains the mailing list, which contains the address and names of the other nodes on the network. The worm, after getting access to this list, sends a copy of itself to all those nodes.

As a result of this uninterrupted transfer over the network, the speed of the network reduces considerably, because of the consumption of the network resources like network buffers, disk capacity etc. If it continues further, the entire network may be brought down and services to the legal users may be denied.

We can safeguard against the computer worms either by preventing their creation, which can be achieved by having very strong security and protection policies or by preventing the spreading of the worms by introducing various *check points* in the communication paths.

10.3.2 Computer Viruses

A computer virus is an intentionally written part of a program.

It can directly infect the code and data unlike 'computer worm', which can consume the network resources only.

Depending upon the place in memory where the virus resides or depending upon what the virus affects, there are several types of viruses like:

- Boot sector infector
- Command processor infectors
- File specific infectors
- Memory resident infectors

The virus code infects a program by *appending* it to the program, by *deleting* some part of the program, by *inserting* itself in the main body of the program or by *replacing* the original code partially or completely.

To write a virus program one needs to have a great knowledge of the entire system. Generally virus programs creep in along with a game or some other interesting utility. When the user executes such a utility program the virus code also gets executed and gradually infects the entire system.

Now-a-days several 'virus detection' programs are widely available. They are, in general, automatically invoked immediately after the system is booted. They monitor all the memory and I/O operations for guarding against any improper behavior.

As far as virus programs and its disastrous affects are considered, 'prevention is better than cure'. Once a virus program has damaged some data on the computer it cannot be retrieved at any cost. The best way to prevent the virus programs from entering your system is to purchase legal software from genuine dealers. One needs to be very careful about the free software and trial versions.

10.4 Principles of Security Design

The following points are to be taken into consideration while designing a secure system.

- Only the essential privileges, which are necessary for getting executed, should be granted to every process.
- As a default, no access should be granted to any user. With this approach a legitimate user may be denied access sometimes. However, this is less dangerous than granting access to illegitimate users.
- The design of a secure system should be simple, easy to understand and easy to use for the users.
- Security should be built as an integral part of the system without making it an additional new feature. Also, security should be present at all layers of the system including the lowest ones.

10.4.1 Authentication

It is a process of verifying whether a person is a legitimate user or not. Authentication, in a centralized environment, may be achieved using one of the following:

- Password
- Artifact (possessed only by that user)
- Human characteristics of the user

Password

It is the most commonly used scheme to achieve authentication. Every legitimate user is given a login name by the system administrator in general, which the user needs to type in for logging into the system. After entering the login name he is required to key in his password, which he can choose on his own.

Although there are no fixed conditions for choosing a password, a general convention is followed everywhere, which is to choose a password whose length is in between 6-8 characters. It is a clever approach to choose a password that is a combination of both upper and lower case letters and also containing some numeric values. Many systems allow even special characters like @, #.

Normally, the password entered is not echoed on the

computer screen. Also, the password is stored in an encrypted form in the password file so that even if someone gets access to that file he/she cannot decipher the user passwords.

Artifacts

Some systems, for example ATM, make use of artifacts such as electronic smart cards. The user needs to supply the genuine artifact in order that he logs on to the system. In some systems, where more security is needed, this method is coupled with the use of a password.

Human Characteristics

Comparatively, this is the most secure method to achieve authentication. The finger prints, patterns in the retina of the eye, facial characteristics etc. of the user may be used very effectively to check for the authenticity. Similar to the previous cases here also the user will be having a login name and upon entering it he needs to give his finger prints (or something else depending upon the system's procedures).

The system then compares these prints with those that are present in its database. The user can successfully login if there is a match. Apart from these physiological characteristics, the behavioural characteristics like voice pattern of the user, signature analysis, timing of keystrokes etc. may also be used to check for the authenticity.

10.5 Protection Mechanisms

Protection plays a very crucial role in a multiuser environment, where several users will be making concurrent use of the computer resources such as CPU, memory etc. It is the duty of the operating system to provide a mechanism that protects each process from others.

All the items that require protection in a multiuser environment are known as *objects* and those that want to access these objects are known as *subjects*. The operating system grants different 'access rights' to different subjects.

These rights may include *read*, *write*, *execute*, *append*, *delete* etc.

10.5.1 Domain

A domain is a combination of different objects and a set of different 'access rights' that can be granted to different subjects to operate on each of these objects. An operating system maintains several such domains with different combinations of access rights. The user processes can execute in one of those domains and can access the objects in that domain according to the access rights given to those objects.

Figure 10.1 illustrates this concept.

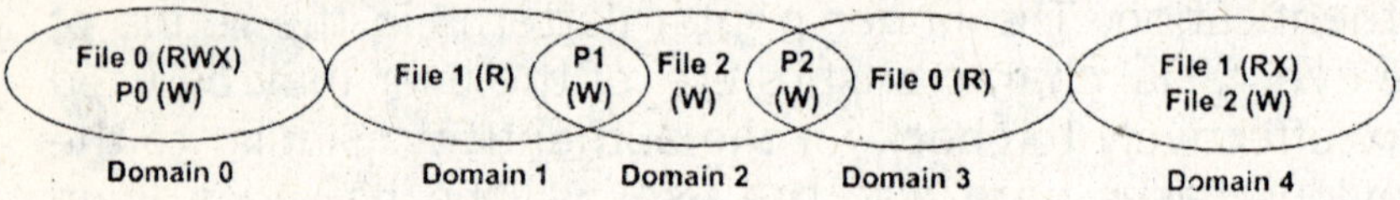

Figure 10.1 *Protection domain*

A user process executing in *domain 0* has access to read from, write into and execute the *file 0* and can write to printer *P0*. Similarly, the process executing in *domain 1* has access to read from *file 1*. The printer *P1* is common to both *domain 1* and *domain 2*. The processes executing in *domain 1* and *domain 2* both can have access to printer *P1*.

In matrix form, the above figure can be represented as shown in figure 10.2.

During the execution of a process, it may become necessary for it to access an object, which is in another domain. If it has a right to access that object it switches to the new domain and accesses that file. This process is known as *domain switching*.

10.5.2 Implementation of Access Matrix

The access matrix can be implemented by using either *access control lists* or *capability lists*.

Objects → Domain ↓	File 0	File 1	File 2	Printer 0	Printer 1	Printer 2
0	RWX			W		
1		R			W	
2			W		W	W
3	R					W
4		RX	W			

Figure 10.2 *Protection matrix*

In ACL, the data is stored by *column* by the operating system. The information about the users and their access rights for each file is maintained by the operating system. The empty entries are discarded.

In capability lists, the access control matrix is sliced horizontally by a row. This implies that the operating system will have to maintain for each user a list of all the objects that the user can access and the ways in which he can access them.

A combination of ACL and capability list techniques may also be used to design protection mechanisms.

10.5.3 Encryption

It is one of the most powerful and important tools of protection. The process of encryption involves two steps: encryption of the original data into some other form about which nothing is known to the third person and decryption of the data into the original form from the encrypted form.

The most commonly used methods to achieve encryption are: *transposition ciphers* and *substitution ciphers*.

In transposition ciphers, the letters in the original message are not changed; only the order in which they are contained in the original message gets changed. For example, consider that the message 'it is raining' needs to be encrypted. It will become 'gniniar si ti' in the encrypted form using a particular form of transposition ciphers algorithm.

The set of characters in the encrypted form will be different from the original ones if we use substitution ciphers. Every letter may be replaced by its previous alphabet, for instance. Now the message 'it is raining' would become, after encryption, 'hs hr qzhmhmf'.

It is very easy to implement these ciphers for characters. The varied forms of these algorithms can be used to encrypt bit steams. For instance, a predetermined bit stream may be added to the bits in the original stream at a particular position to obtain the encrypted message. The same bit steam is subtracted at the destination so that the original stream is obtained. This addition and subtraction may be accomplished with the help of simple adder and subtractor circuits.

The key idea behind the encryption schemes is that the encryption process must be restorable. Means, once we encrypt the original message to a different form, there should be a way to restore it to the original form.

Review Questions

1. When can a system be declared secure?
2. What are the different threats to security?
3. How can a user be authenticated?
4. How does a computer worm spread from one place to another?
5. What is a computer virus?
6. What are the various protection mechanisms?
7. What is a domain of protection?
8. What is an access matrix?
9. Explain the concept of encryption?
10. What are the different methods to achieve encryption?

CHAPTER

11

Secondary Storage Management

Introduction

Nearly all computers make use of disks as the secondary storage devices. The major advantage of disks over magnetic tapes is that disks are random in nature unlike magnetic tapes, which are sequential access devices. Also, disks offer a large storage capacity. In this chapter, we begin with a discussion about disk hardware. We progress studying various disk scheduling algorithms. We talk about disk management also.

11.1 Disk Hardware

All real disks are organized into cylinders. A cylinder is constituted by all tracks that can be accessed without any net movement in the read-write head's position.

Information on the disk can be accessed with the help of the drive number, the surface, the track and the sector. *Information is stored in the sector on a disk*. A sector can be defined as the smallest unit of information. The number of sectors per track varies from 8 to 32. *The number of bytes that can be stored in a sector is the same for all the sectors irrespective of whether they are close to the hub or to the outer rim*. The time to read from or write to a disk block consists of 3 parts. The seek time (the time taken to move the read write head to the correct track), the *rotational delay* (the time to arrive at the correct sector) and the actual *transfer time*.

11.2 Disk Space Management

As said earlier in this chapter, disks serve as the main medium for storing files. A file can be defined as a collection of related information stored on a secondary device under a name. Means, a file can be viewed as a collection of bytes stored in certain memory locations. Since all these bytes represent the information related to a common specific program or job, they have to be linked together in some way or other. The simplest and easiest way to provide this linkage is to store the file in continuous memory locations.

However, this technique is not much advantageous because it creates problems if the file grows in size. The entire file needs to be moved to another location on the disk if a file increases in size. Hence, most file systems follow another strategy to store files, which is to divide the file into a number of blocks and to store each block in a specific location on the disk. This technique proved to be more advantageous because allocating another block would suffice to deal with the problem of increased file size. These blocks may be chained together in one of the following ways:

11.2.1 Block Linkage

In this method, one word in each block is used as a pointer to the next block. The entry for this file in the user level directory is a pointer to the first block of the file. Though the implementation of this method seems to be simple, it has a specific disadvantage, which is the large number of disc accesses needed to find the end of the file. Since each block points to only the next block all the blocks need to be passed through to arrive at the end of the file.

This disadvantage may be overcome by making the file entry in the user level directory point to the end of the file in addition to the beginning.

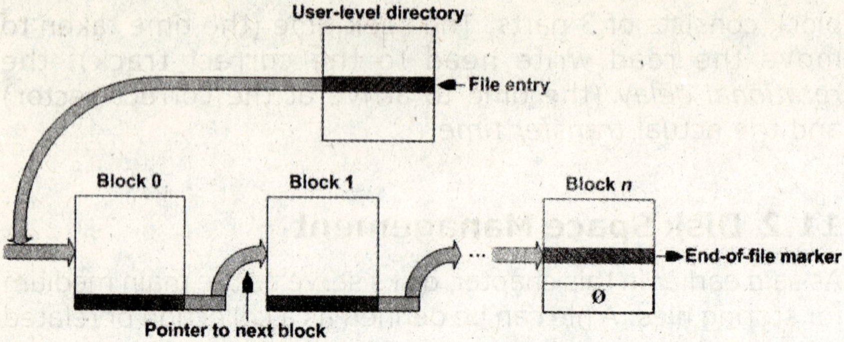

Figure 11.1 *Linked file blocks*

The same concept of linking the blocks can be implemented with the help of a file map in which each block is represented by a single word. The file entry in the user level directory points to a location in the file map, which represents the first block of the file. This location, in turn, points to the location in the map, which represents the second block of the file and so on. A null pointer (Ø) represents the end of the file. This appears to be an indirect version of the previous method.

Similar to the previous method, the access to a file, whose blocks are linked using the file map method, needs to be sequential. Since the number of locations in the file map is equal to the number of blocks that the file occupies, the size of the file map will be large and it is for this reason that the file map is stored on the disk as a separate file and is brought into the main memory one block at a time as required.

As can be observed from figure 11.2, the blocks used are 2, 4, 1 and 8.

11.2.2 Index Block

The linking methods we have seen previously suffer from a main demerit in that they require more number of disk accesses to arrive at a specific block, since the file access method must be sequential. More number of disk accesses means more number of head movements and corresponding rotational delays. This demerit can be overcome if

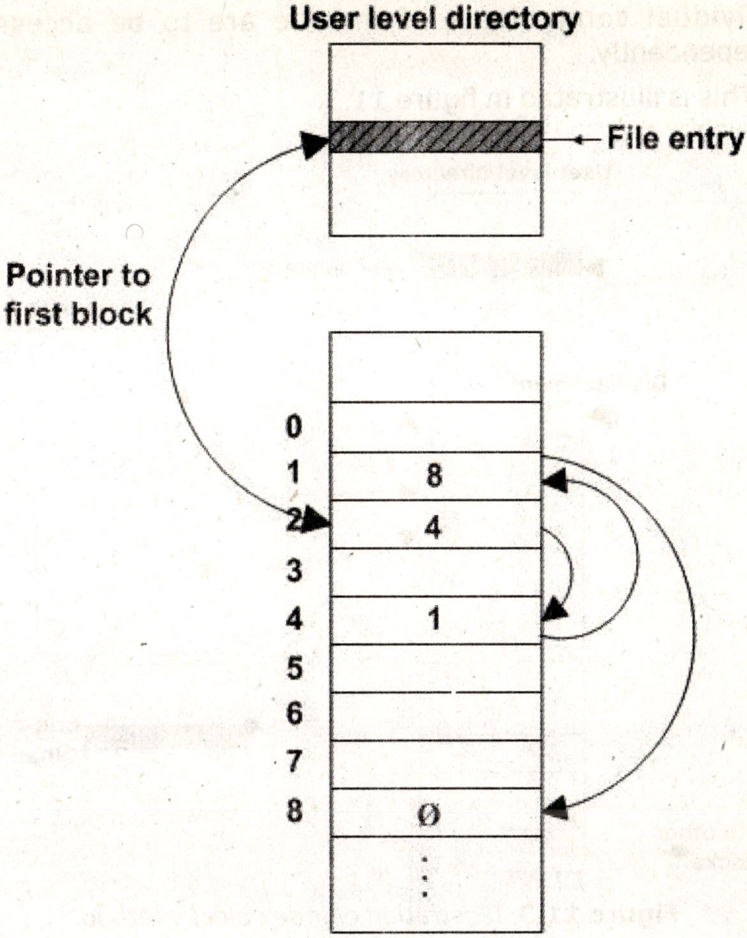

Figure 11.2 *File map*

the file access can be random. This can be achieved with the help of index blocks which are used to store the linkage pointers for each file. The size of each index block is limited and hence a large file might require many blocks, which are linked together.

Using index blocks any block may be accessed at random if the name of the file and the offset of the block in the index block are specified. If any block in the middle of the file is deleted or added, the entire index block needs to be modified since the displacement values of each block vary. However, this method of providing a link between the blocks of a file proved to be efficient for the cases in which the individual components of the file are to be accessed independently.

This is illustrated in figure 11.3.

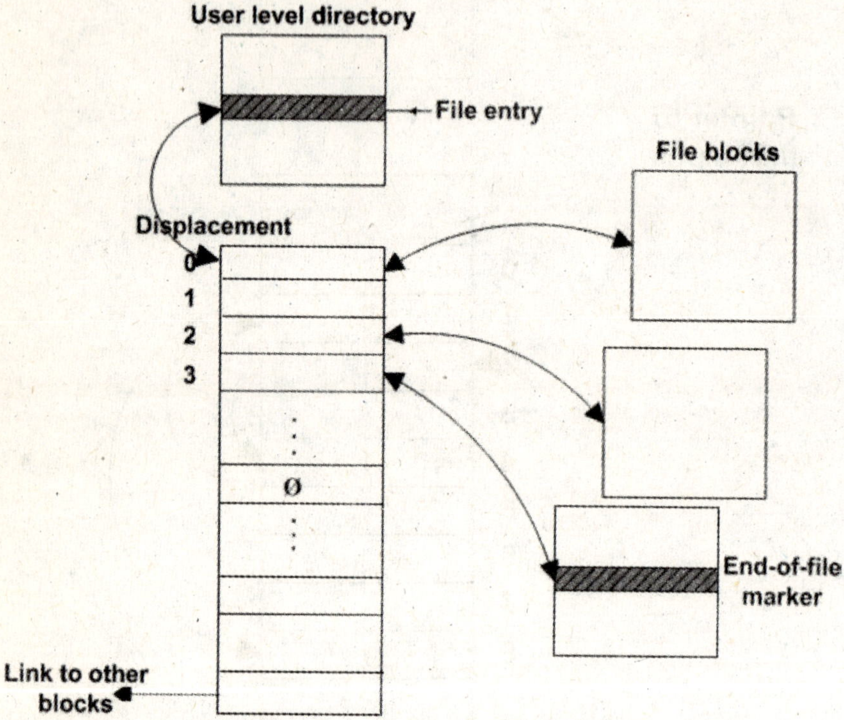

Figure 11.3 *Illustration of index block method*

11.2.3 Block Size

Choosing a proper block size is an important function of disk management. In a previous chapter, while studying the paging scheme, we discussed that the page size plays a very important role in memory management. The size of the page should not be too large or too small because in both the cases the problem of fragmentation arises. Similarly, the block size should also be properly chosen so that the disk space is not wasted. The most commonly used block sizes are 512, 1k and 2k bytes. The block size and the sector size need not be the same. For instance, if the sector size is 1k bytes and the block size is 2k bytes then always

2 consecutive sectors are read from the disk and are treated as a single unit.

11.3 Disk Scheduling

The necessity of scheduling the requests to access the disk comes because of the competition held among several jobs. The jobs depend heavily upon the disk for program loading and for I/O. The main goal of disk scheduling is to reduce the mean seek time. In this section, we study various disk scheduling algorithms.

11.3.1 FCFS Scheduling

It is the simplest form of disk scheduling. The requests are serviced in the order they arrive in the queue. This algorithm is very easy to implement. However, it doesn't reduce the average seek time effectively. For example, consider a disk having 20 cylinders. Let the queue be formed with the requests to access tracks 2, 18, 7, 15, 4, 13 in that order. If the read-write head is initially at track 16, it will move first to track 2 and from there to 18, 7, 15, 4 and then finally to track 13. This schedule can be illustrated diagrammatically as shown in figure 11.4.

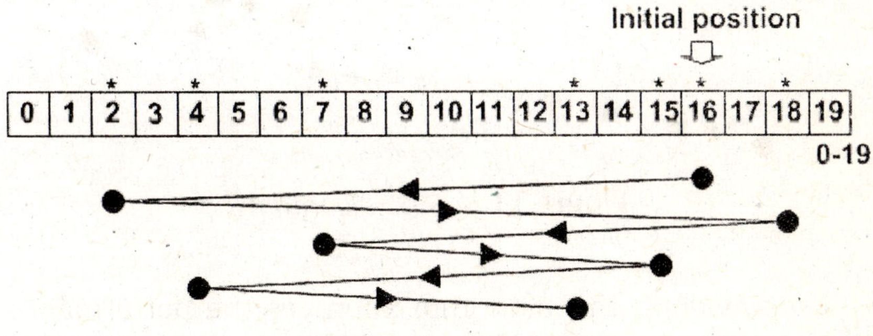

Figure 11.4 *FIFO algorithm*

As is evident, there are large swings from one track to another. Certainly, this type of scheduling doesn't offer a good average seek time.

11.3.2 SSTF Scheduling

As defined earlier, seek time is the time taken for the read-write head to move from the current position to next track. This indicates that seek time is proportional to the track difference between requests. That means, the seek time can be reduced considerably if the head is moved from the current position to the closest track. And this forms the basis for *shortest seek time first* scheduling algorithm, which selects the request with minimum seek time from the queue.

As an example, consider the same queue as earlier. The track closest to the initial position (16) is 15. So, the head moves to track 15 from the initial position. Now, the tracks 13 and 18 are closer to the current head position. Since the track difference between 15 and 13 is 2 and that between 15 and 18 is 3, the next request to be serviced is 13. And, going this way, the sequence would be 18, 7, 4, and 2. The schematic representation of this algorithm is as shown in figure 11.5.

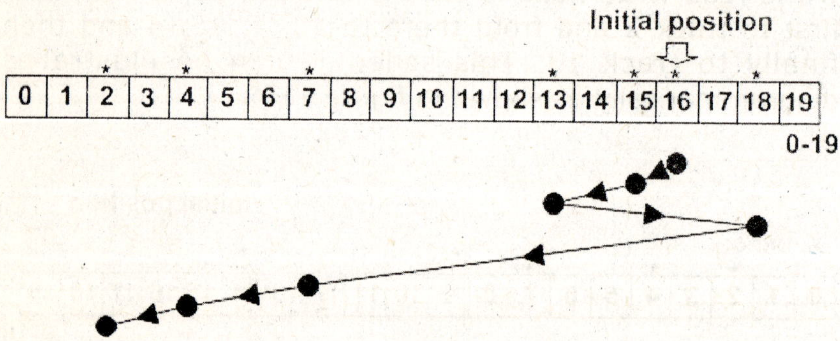

Figure 11.5 *SSTF algorithm*

As is evident, this algorithm improves the performance of the system comparatively. As can be observed, this algorithm resembles the shortest job first algorithm of CPU scheduling. And similar to that algorithm SSTF algorithm also causes the same severe problem, starvation.

Starvation in disk scheduling can be illustrated like this: Suppose that the head is initially at track 10 and that there are 2 requests waiting in the queue to access tracks 14 and 50. Since the track 14 is close to the head's current position that request is serviced first making the request for track 50 wait. While the request for track 14 is being serviced another request for track 19 might arrive. Then, that request is serviced making the request at track 50 wait again. Theoretically, it may happen that requests close to track 14 arrive in a sequence and the request for track 50 wait indefinitely.

11.3.3 Scan and C-Scan Scheduling

The concept used in scheduling the elevator in tall buildings can be used to implement another algorithm known as scan algorithm. In the use of elevator, requests come at random from various floors. The elevator continues moving in the same direction attending the requests in that direction.

If the microprocessor keeping track of the requests notices that there are no more requests in that direction it switches the direction and the elevator now moves in the other direction.

Now let us see how the scan algorithm works. The head starts at one end of the disk and moves towards the other end servicing each request in that direction. If there are no requests in the current direction then the head reverses its direction. This algorithm makes use of a bit to indicate the direction. If the bit is set i.e., if the bit is 1 it indicates 'up' and if the bit is 0 it indicates 'down' (towards '0').

To illustrate this algorithm let us consider the previous example in which the head is initially at track 16. Suppose that the head is moving towards 0. Then the next request that will be serviced is 15 and then 13. Continuing this way, the sequence will be 7, 4, and 2. At track 2, the head notices that there are no requests in the current direction. Then the direction bit is set and the head moves in the opposite direction. Now the request for the tack 18 is serviced. Figure 11.6 illustrates this algorithm. However, there is a problem with this algorithm too. What happens if a request arrives in the queue for a track just behind the head? The request has to wait until the head reverses its direction at the end of the disk and reaches it.

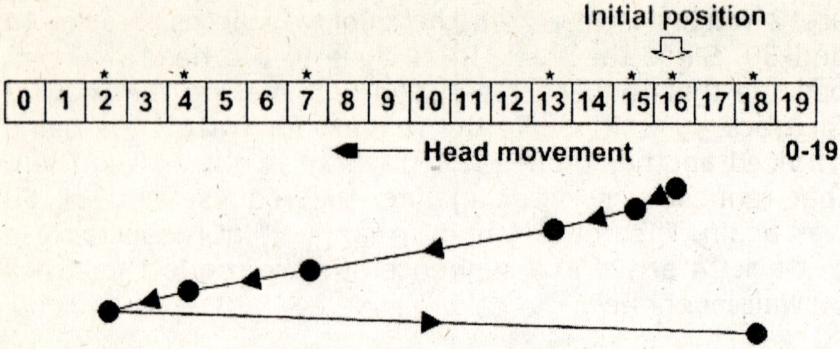

Figure 11.6 *Scan algorithm*

To make the waiting time uniform we go for *C-Scan* (Circular Scan) scheduling. This algorithm is similar to the scan algorithm. Here also, if the head moves from one end of the disk to the other end it attends to the requests in that direction. The modification in this algorithm is that the head, after reaching one end, returns to the beginning immediately without attending any requests in the reverse direction. This algorithm treats the disk to be circular.

These are various types of most commonly used disk scheduling algorithms. The performance of any algorithm is greatly influenced by such factors like the file allocation method, the allocation of the directories etc.

A disk scheduling algorithm is written as a distinct module of the operating system. This module can be replaced by another one if necessary. Although there are several quantitative approaches to decide which algorithm works well it is always the best approach to code a specific algorithm and link it as a separate module to the OS and test it in real time. If it proves not to be optimal it can be replaced with another module.

11.4 Disk Errors and Bad Blocks

A disk becomes ready for use when it is formatted. This formatting is of two types: *physical formatting* and *logical formatting*. The disks are physically formatted in the factory itself and the operating system formats the disks logically.

The physical formatting involves dividing the disk into several sectors. And the logical formatting writes a blank directory into the disk for storing certain essential information. Now, bad blocks are those which are unreadable and unwritable. These bad blocks are detected when the disk is formatted and are replaced by the spare blocks, which are kept away from the user processes. The disk controller keeps track of these spare tracks and the bad blocks.

Disk errors are of various types like programming errors, seek errors and controller errors etc. Programming errors are said to occur when the controller is directed to write to or read from a non existent sector. The controller checks the parameters associated with the request and it complains if they are found to be invalid. Seek errors result due to the mechanical problems in the arm. These problems may make the arm arrive at a wrong sector thereby causing seek errors.

Generally, seek errors are corrected automatically by the controllers. And the controller errors are caused when the controller denies accepting any commands. Sometimes a bug in the functioning of the controller may make it enter into a loop. As a result the controller gets stuck without accepting any new commands. The controller is reset to make it come out of the loop and work properly.

11.5 Backup

Just now we have studied that the data in the bad blocks is usually lost. Many times such a loss causes disastrous results whatever may be the approach we follow to deal with the problem of bad blocks. So, it is always a wise idea to backup the files at regular intervals.

Having a backup of the data can simply be understood as producing duplicate copies of the data. These copies are generally stored on a backing store or on magnetic tapes, which are permanent storage devices.

When a specific file is found corrupted, say, because of a virus attack, and the damage is estimated to be incorrigible then that file can be deleted from the memory and in its place its copy version can be loaded from the secondary storage device.

Although it is a better approach to have a backup of the entire file system at regular intervals, say 1 week or 1 month, it consumes a lot of time. Hence, the best way is to dump only those files that have been modified since the last dump. The assistance of 'archive bit' is taken to decide whether a specific file is modified or not.

11.6 Cache

The delay in arriving at the correct track on the disk due to mechanical problems in the arm severely affects the speed at which data is read from or written to the sectors. Disc accesses are many times (nearly 105 times) slower than memory accesses. Hence, it is a good idea to keep the number of disc accesses as low as possible. This can be achieved by making use of 'block cache'.

A cache can be defined as a collection of disc blocks that are stored in main memory. A block is kept in the cache if it proves to be an important block that might be needed by the programmer a little later. When a read request is made the cache is searched for the required block(s). If it is found, the request can be serviced without a disc access. Otherwise, the block is read from the disc into the cache first and then to where it is needed. Any subsequent requests for the same block can be serviced directly from cache.

For currently available drives, the seek time is several times larger than the actual transfer time. Hence, when the arm is properly moved on to the correct track reading the entire track or a single sector doesn't matter much in terms of transfer time. Some controllers make use of this fact and they instruct the head to read the entire track instead of simply one sector and store this entire track in cache. This type of caching is known as track-at-a-time caching. Whenever a reference to a sector belonging to the same track is made, that sector can be read directly from the cache.

Review Questions

1. What is the advantage of secondary storage medium?
2. Explain the structure of a disk.
3. Why is disk scheduling necessary?
4. Explain various disk scheduling algorithms in detail.
5. What is a bad block?
6. What are the different types of disk errors?
7. How can two blocks be linked to each other?
8. What is the necessity to back up the data?
9. What is the significance of caching?
10. What is track-at-a-time caching?

CHAPTER 12

Distributed Systems

Introduction

This chapter talks about network fundamentals. It discusses various advantages offered by distributed systems. It also explains network hardware and other networking aspects and then various network topologies and switching strategies. And, finally it talks about the OSI reference model. Please note that the terms network and distributed system are used interchangeably in this chapter.

12.1 What Is A Distributed System?

Imagine this situation: There are two computers at sites A and B. The computer at site B has a printer connected to it. A person working on the computer at site A wants to get the printout of a particular file from the printer at site B. Then he saves that file in a floppy, takes it to the computer at site B, opens it and then takes the printout. This entire process takes nearly 10 minutes if sites A and B are adjacent rooms. It may take even long if the distance between sites A and B is larger.

Now, imagine that the computers at site A and site B are linked together by some means and the file is transferred to the printer via that link. Now, the delay reduces to a great extent. And, this idea of providing a link among several processors situated at various sites, which do not share a common memory or a clock, forms the basis for distributed systems.

Definition: A distributed system is a collection of several loosely coupled processors interconnected by a high speed communication network. These processors may vary in size, speed, performance and other issues.

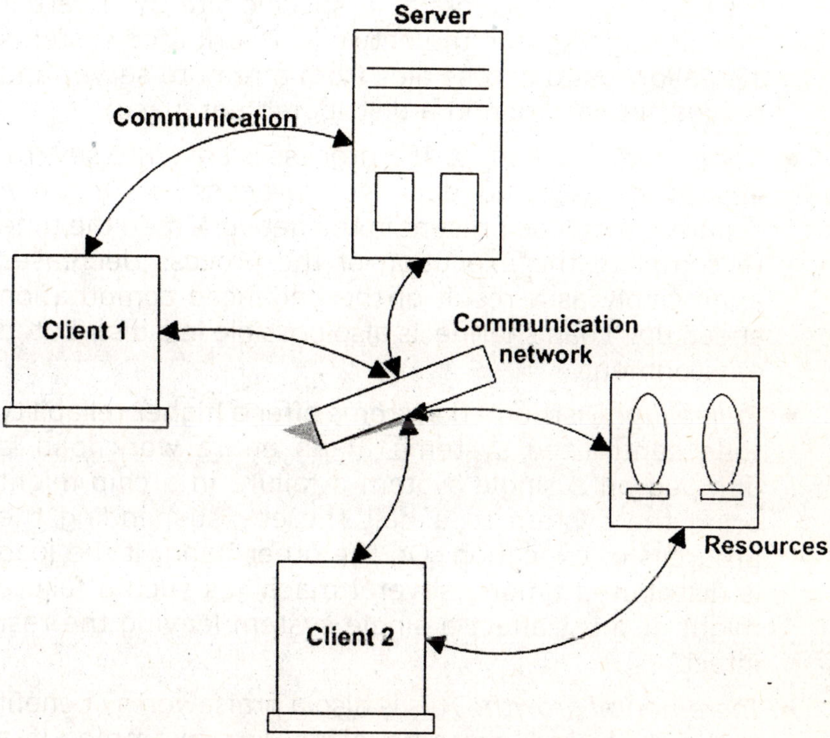

Figure 12.1 *Distributed system*

12.2 The Drive

The driving force behind the development of distributed systems is the significance of the advantages of distributed computing. The major advantages of distributed systems can be short listed as below.

- *Economy:* The price-performance ratio that the distributed systems offer is much better than that could be obtained through centralized systems. For example, if a processor costs fifty dollars then it is a good idea to purchase two processors and interconnect them forming a distributed system than to purchase a single processor of relatively high speed, which costs hundred dollars.
- *Resource sharing:* As we have seen at the beginning of this chapter, distributed systems allow for sharing the resources available at a specific site by different machines present in the network. Distributed systems also allow us to access files from a remote server and process information in a distributed database.
- *Computation speedup:* If a process is split into several sub processes and each sub process is run on a separate machine present in the network then the time to complete the execution of the process decreases appreciably as a result of the enhanced computation speed up. 'Load sharing' is also possible in a distributed environment.
- *Reliability:* Distributed systems offer a higher reliability than centralized systems. If an entire work load is dumped on a single system a failure in a chip might bring the system to a halt thereby suspending the progress of execution. On the other hand, if the load is distributed among several machines such a failure might at most affect a single system leaving the rest intact.
- *Incremental growth:* This is also a praiseworthy benefit the distributed systems offer. For example, if a company wants to expand the range of operations it is performing and the current mainframe is found to be incapable of managing the entire mayhem then the company might replace the current mainframe with another one of greater capacity or add a second mainframe. None of these possibilities assures a decent system. In a distributed environment, this problem can be managed by simply adding some more processors to the network depending upon the requirement.

- *Communication:* This is the highly perceivable advantage that a common user can enjoy. The interconnection of the processors allows the users (at different sites) to exchange information by sending messages. Also, a single team, whose members are present at various points on the globe, is now able to execute a project by exchanging information among its members with less expenditure of both energy and money.

Although distributed systems offer several advantages there are some disadvantages as well, which proved to be potential.

- The lack of 100% efficient software and the presence of other technological limitations might make the network become saturated and that may sometimes corrupt the messages.
- The idea to make all the data on a distributed system available to every user turns out dangerous when secret information that needs to be guarded against malicious modifications also becomes equally accessible by all users on the network.

12.3 Networking Issues

In this section, we will study the physical and internal aspects of a communication network, which form a vital component of a distributed system.

12.3.1 Physical Aspects / Network Hardware

Basing on *transmission technology* and *scale* all the networks can be categorized into several classes.

- A classification basing on transmission technology results in two types of networks:
  - ¤ Broadcast networks
  - ¤ Point-to-point networks

In broadcast networks, there exists a common communication channel, which is shared by all the machines on the network. The message from source to destination is sent in the form of packets. The address field in the header of the message packet contains the destination address. All the machines in the network receive that packet. The address field is checked at every machine and the packet is processed if it is intended for that machine, otherwise the packet is ignored.

By setting a special column in the header the same packet can be made accessible to all the machines on the network. On the other hand, in point-to-point networks there exist a number of connections between a pair of terminals. That means, there can be more than one path for message at site A to arrive at site B. Hence, *routing algorithms* play a very significant role in point-to-point networks whose purpose is to direct the path for a message so as that it arrives at the destination with much ease.

- A categorization basing on the distance between processors in the network announces two different classes of networks:

  ¤ Local Area Networks (LANs)
  ¤ Wide Area Networks (WANs).

In a local area network, the interprocessor distance ranges from 10 m to 1 km. Generally, LANs are privately owned networks confined to a building or a campus. The error rate in LANs is lower and speed and reliability are higher than that can be obtained in WANs. In order that these higher speed and lower error rate are obtained the linking medium should be of very rich quality. The most commonly used links include twisted pair, broadband coaxial cable and fiber optics. The communication speeds range from 10 megabytes per second to 1 gigabyte per second.

The figure below illustrates a typical local area network.

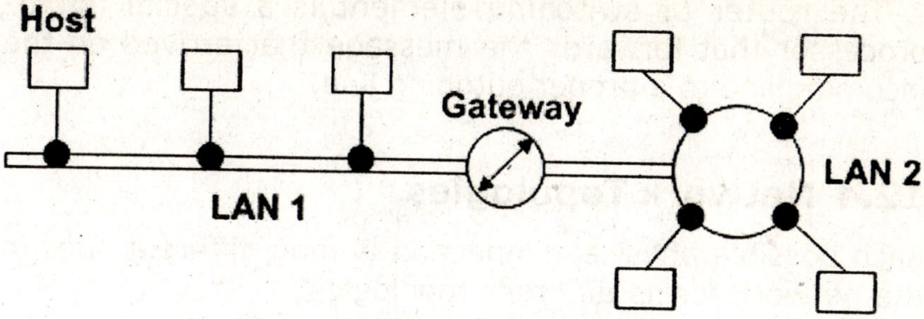

Figure 12.2 *Local area network*

A gateway allows one LAN to interact with another network. Wide area networks interconnect processors, which are separated by distances ranging from 10 km to above 10,000 km. The worldwide network of networks, Internet, is also a type of WAN, which is the developed version of the Arpanet. Since WANs cover a wide geographical area the communication links they make use of are slow and unreliable compared to their LAN counterparts.

The term subnet comes into picture in WANs. A subnet consists of transmission lines to carry messages from one host to another and switching elements or routers to connect two or more transmission lines. The communication links used in WANs include telephone lines microwave links and satellite channels etc.

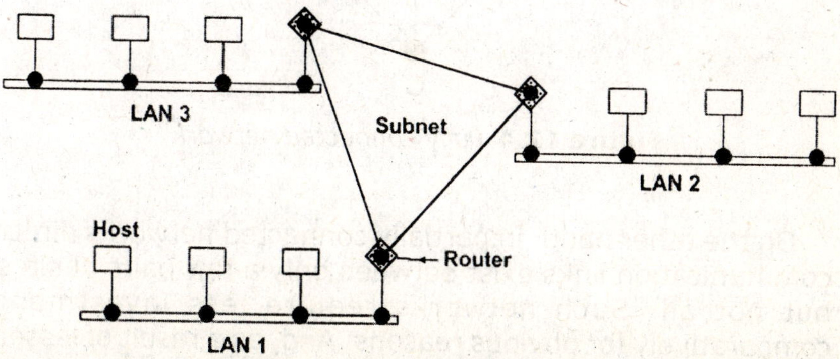

Figure 12.3 *Wide area network*

The router or switching element is a special microprocessor that forwards the message that arrived on the incoming line to a proper outgoing line.

12.4 Network Topologies

Each possible physical connection among different sites in the network forms different topologies.

12.4.1 Fully connected and partially connected networks

In a fully connected network, there exists a direct link between every pair of sites in the network. This direct connection makes these systems highly reliable. However, this reliability is obtained with increased expenditure. Since, there exists a link between every two hosts the failure in a single link doesn't affect the entire network. A fully connected network is shown in figure 12.4.

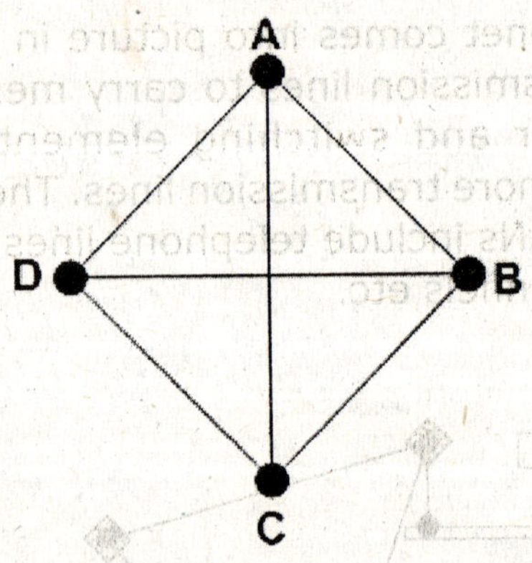

Figure 12.4 *Fully connected network*

On the other hand, in partially connected networks direct communication links exist between only a few pairs of sites but not all. Such networks require less investment comparatively for obvious reasons. And, as a result of lesser links present in the network, the reliability in this type of networks will not be very high.

Now observe figure 12.5. If the link between the sites B and E breaks there will be no means for the site D to communicate with A, B or C. That means a failure in one link affects the entire system to a considerable extent.

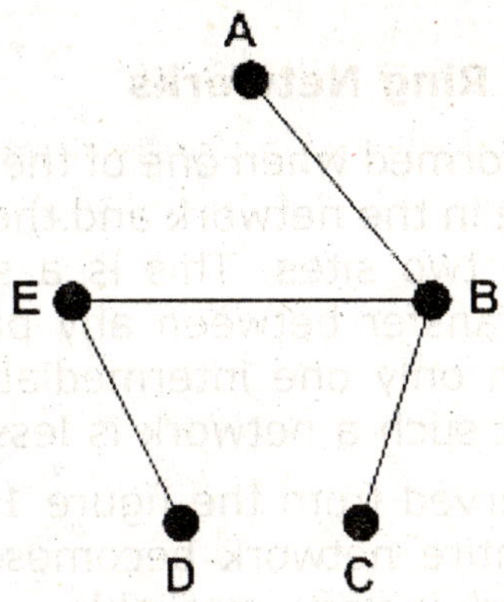

Figure 12.5 *Partially connected network*

12.4.2 Hierarchical Networks

The name itself indicates that the sites in this type of network are arranged in the form of a tree. This type of network is also not a much efficient and reliable one because a failure in one link makes low-level sites lose contact with the high-level ones. For example, consider the network illustrated in figure 12.6.

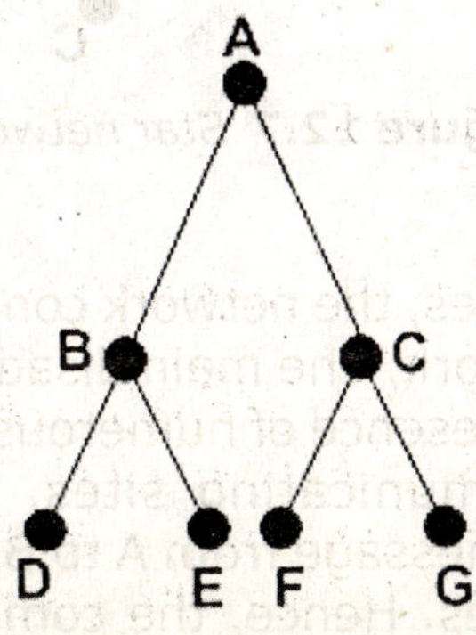

Figure 12.6 *Hierarchical network*

A is the parent of B and C, whose siblings are D, E and F, G respectively. If the link between A and B fails D and E cannot communicate with the other wing of sites. The advantage of hierarchical networks is that they require less initial investment.

12.4.3 Star and Ring Networks

A star network is formed when one of the sites is connected to every other site in the network and there exists no other link between any two sites. This is a simple network in which message transfer between any pair of terminals is accomplished with only one intermediate node. Also, the cost to implement such a network is less.

As can be observed from the figure 12.7, if the central node fails, the entire network becomes obsolete. Hence, this type of network is very unreliable.

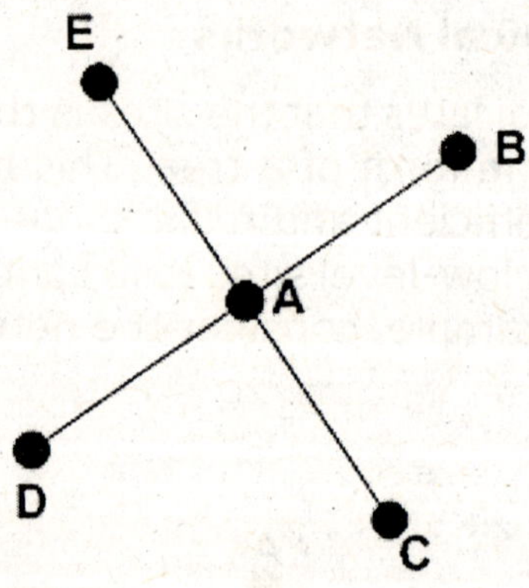

Figure 12.7 *Star network*

As the name implies, the network configuration resembles a ring in a ring network. The main disadvantage of this type of networks is the presence of numerous intermediate nodes between two communicating sites. If the ring is uni-directional, then a message from A to B has to pass through 4 intermediate nodes. Hence, the communication cost will be high.

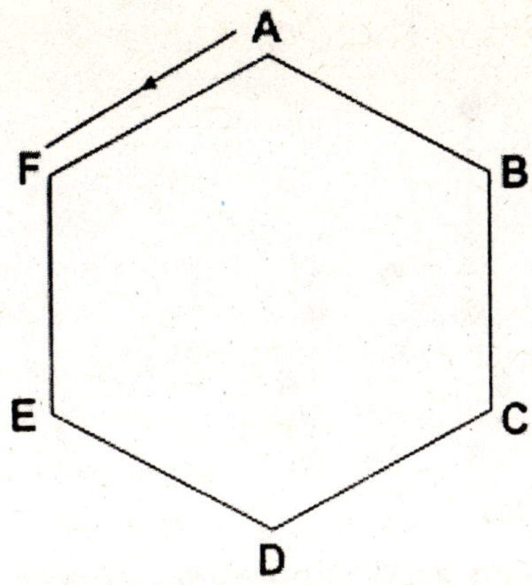

Figure 12.8 *Ring network*

12.4.4 Bus Networks

In this type of networks, the communication link is organized in the form of a straight line or a ring to which all the nodes are attached. The most commonly and widely used LAN-Ethernet is built basing upon this bus model. Bus model networks are shown in figure 12.9.

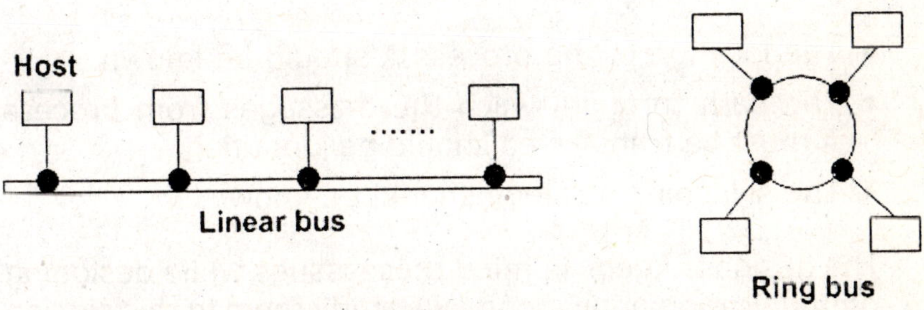

Figure 12.9 *Bus network*

There are still several other types of topologies like intersecting ring networks, irregular networks, and hybrid networks etc., which are not very frequently used.

12.5 Internal Aspects

In the previous section, we have studied the physical appearance and interconnectivity patterns of networks. In

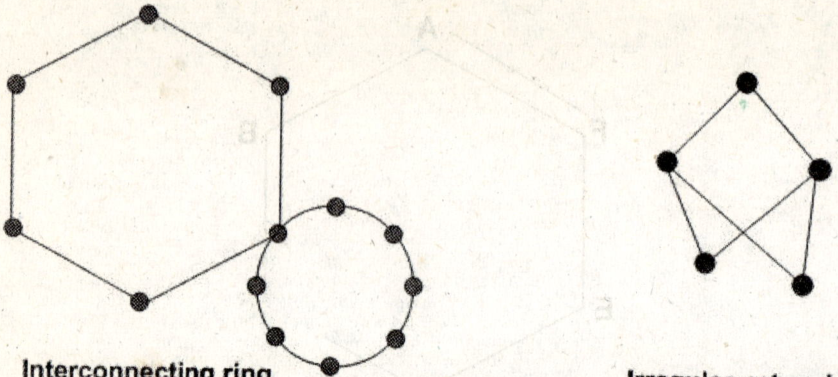

Figure 12.10 *Other types of networks*

this section, we turn our attention towards the actual side, the internals of a network.

As we know, the main purpose of establishing a network interconnecting several sites is to allow different processes at different sites to communicate with each other. For example, if site A wants to communicate with another process at site B the following sequence of steps has to take place:

- The location of the process A should be known.
- The path through which the messages from process A must be transferred should be identified.
- The switching strategy should be known.

The designer keeps in mind these issues while designing a communication network and we study them in this section thoroughly.

12.5.1 Identifying the location and name resolution

Address Location: Every host in the network is identified by a name, and every process bears an identification number. The <*host name, process-id*> makes a unique pair and this pair is used to identify a specific process to communicate with. The computers have ease in dealing with numbers than names. Hence, there should be a mechanism, which makes this name to number translation. This mechanism is

DNS (domain name service), which is always consulted by the kernel of a system to know the Internet address of a specific process. The entire Internet is divided into a number of domains each of which contains thousands of hosts. Each domain can be subdivided into subdomains. The most famous domains are .com, .edu and .net etc.

The clear picture: If a process A wants to communicate with a process B present on another host, first it fetches the name of the host on which the process resides and the id number of that process. Then the kernel of the system containing process A interacts with the DNS to find out the 'Internet address', commonly known as the IP address of the host of process B. Then a connection is established between the 2 hosts and finally the processes A and B communicate with each other.

12.5.2 Routing

The routing strategy determines how a connection is to be setup between two hosts. To achieve higher reliability several alternate paths need to be maintained in the network. The presence of these alternate paths makes it necessary to route a packet. There are three commonly used routing strategies:

- *Fixed Routing:* A path, usually the shortest path, between two sites is specified permanently in advance, which doesn't alter unless any network failure forces for the alternation. The information about the paths from one node to another is maintained in a table, which is referenced to establish a path to a new mode.
- *Virtual Circuit:* A path is selected for every session separately. Hence, different sessions of communication between two processes might use different paths.
- *Dynamic Routing:* This allows the processes to communicate with each other using different paths during a single session. A path is decided only when a message is sent. Hence, different messages of the same session may travel in different paths.

12.5.3 Switching Strategies

The job of a switching strategy is to connect different pairs of communicating processes. The commonly used techniques to establish such a connection are:

- *Circuit Switching:* In this technique, a path is established between every pair of communicating processes at the beginning of the session and is destroyed only when the processes indicate the end of their communication. That means the allocated physical link is held by the processes until they complete their communication and no other process can use that link during that period.
- *Message Switching:* The link established between two processes is temporary in this scheme and its life time is equal to the duration of one message transfer. The data is divided into messages and each message contains some specific information like the destination address etc.
- *Packet Switching:* In this case, the message is split into several units of fixed length, which are known as packets. Each of these packets contains some important details like: the source address, the destination address, packet number etc. Each of these packets may travel in different paths and the original message is reconstructed with the help of the information present in each of the packets.

So far, we have discussed the plain case in which the physical link between a pair of processes is used only by those two processes, at least until a session is over. But depending upon the topology used a link may connect more than two sites and hence there is a possibility for simultaneous transmission of data on this link by different sites. This simultaneous transmission leads to 'collisions', the result of which is scrambled and discardable information. To deal with the problem of collisions there are several techniques developed, and CSMA/CD, token passing are a few of them.

12.5.4 CSMA / CD

In this technique, a particular site continuously listens to sense whether some other station is transmitting messages over the link. If the link is found to be free it sends its messages. Otherwise, it waits a random amount of time and then repeats the same procedure. If two stations start transmitting exactly at the same time they detect a collision and stop transmitting, wait for some period and repeat the previous steps. This scheme works well on systems with less number of hosts. If the number of machines on the network increases the number of collisions also increases and the performance of the system decreases.

12.5.5 Token Passing

This scheme is used usually in a ring network (IEEE 802.5). A token, which is a special bit pattern, is circulated around the entire ring continuously when the sites are idle. Any site that wants to transmit using the channel needs to seize this token first. After it completes transmitting its data it regenerates the token. The performance of a networking system that adopts this scheme remains constant at all times. However, adding a new system increases the time that a site waits for the token.

12.6 Network Software Structures

In the early days of computer networks, designs were made keeping the hardware as the main object of concern. But now the scenario has been changed. The importance of network software grew incredibly which is playing a praiseworthy role in simplifying the network complexity.

To reduce the design complexity and consequent problems, the networks are organized in multiple layers. The number of layers, the name of each layer and the function of each layer vary from one network to another.

The communication takes place only between *peer* layers and is controlled by a protocol designed for those layers. However, in reality, no two peer layers on different machines can interact with each other directly. Instead, each layer passes the data and the relevant control information to the layer immediately below it. The last layer puts this data on the physical link, which connects the two machines.

As said earlier, the communication between peer layers is controlled by a protocol designed specially for those layers. That means each layer has a protocol and the number of protocols is equal to the number of layers. All these protocols constitute the protocol stack, which controls the data flow in the entire system.

12.7 Reference Model

In this section, we briefly study the OSI reference model, which was developed by international standards organization (ISO). Open Systems Interconnection (OSI) model, which is illustrated in figure 12.11, has seven layers.

The functions of all the seven layers are described below:

- *Physical layer:* This layer is responsible for transmitting raw bits over a communication channel. Its job is to make sure that a bit 0 sent by one side is accepted at the other side as 0 and not as 1.
- *Data link layer:* This layer defines the boundaries of data frames and instructs the sender to split the data in such a way that it fits into these frames. This layer also corrects any errors found on these frames.
- *Network layer:* It controls the operation of the subnet. Its main function is to route the packets over the network.
- *Transport layer:* Its function is to receive data from session layer and pass it to the network layer splitting it into small units.
- *Session layer:* The session layer allows the establishment of sessions between two different processes. A session layer is used to log a user into a remote system.
- *Presentation layer:* This layer is concerned with the syntax and semantics of the information being transmitted. It doesn't simply transmit the data from the upper layer to the layer below it. But it also resolves the differences among various sites in the network.

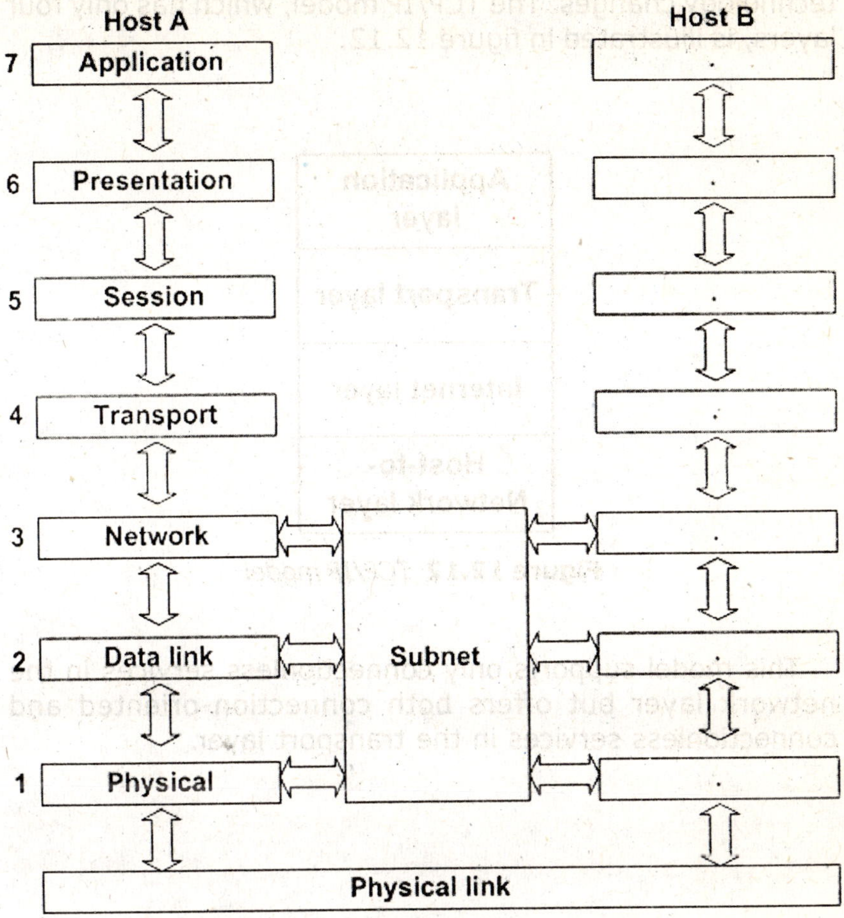

Figure 12.11 *OSI reference model*

- *Application layer:* This layer contains several protocols that are most commonly needed. It deals with file transfer, electronic mail etc.

The other reference model, which is still being used on the Internet, is the *Transmission Control Protocol/Internet Protocol* (TCP/IP) model. This stack has relatively less number of layers because a single layer in the TCP/IP model offers a combination of services. This stack is difficult to implement but is more efficient than the OSI stack. The protocols in the TCP/IP model cannot be replaced as the technology changes. The TCP/IP model, which has only four layers, is illustrated in figure 12.12.

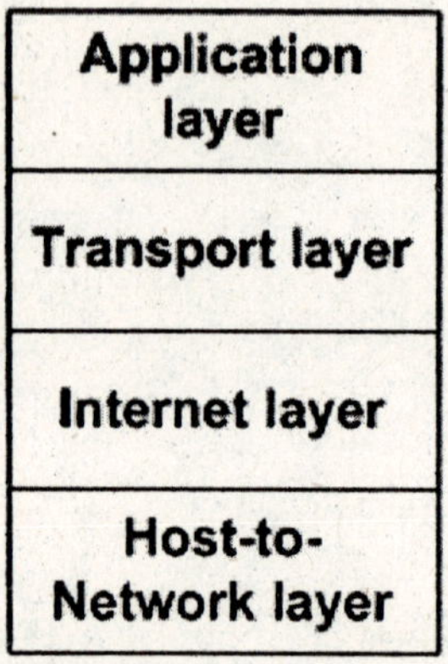

Figure 12.12 *TCP/IP model*

This model supports only connectionless services in the network layer but offers both connection-oriented and connectionless services in the transport layer.

Review Questions

1. What is the advantage of networking two computers?
2. What is a distributed system?
3. List the advantages of a distributed system.
4. What are the different categorizations in networks?
5. Differentiate between LANs and WANs.
6. Explain different network topologies.
7. How can we identify a host in the network?
8. What is meant by routing?
9. Explain various switching techniques.
10. Explain CSMA/CD.
11. How is a token used in a ring network?
12. Explain the OSI reference model.

CHAPTER

13

Distributed Operating Systems

Introduction

The main purpose of this chapter is to discuss the various aspects of distributed-operating systems. We start with a discussion on network-operating systems (NOS). We talk about the various functions of the NOS and later we turn our attention towards the superior layer of software, the distributed-operating system, to get an overview of the salient features and functions of it.

13.1 Network Operating Systems

A network operating system enables the users to access remote resources either by logging into the proper machine or by transferring the data from that machine to their own machines. However, the user needs to be aware of the data location and the multiplicity of machines.

Each machine on the network has a local operating system, which handles the non I/O requests made by the application programs. If the user wants to access data from a remote site he makes the application program release a system call for 'remote read' operation, which can certainly not be handled by the local operating system. Now the network operating system comes into picture, which is organized as a layer above the local operating system.

The NOS has several modules each of which is responsible for a separate action. Below we describe about these modules basing on the client-server model.

13.1.1 Redirection software

The redirection software exists on the client machine whose function is to handle the I/O requests made by the application programs. If the I/O request is for local data the redirection software directs it to the local operating system. And if the request is for remote data it is sent to the remote server. Normally, in the case of a dedicated server, the redirection software is present on the server also because it needs to decide whether the data it is passing is for a local user or remote user.

13.1.2 Communication Management Software

This software also resides on both client station and server. It receives the I/O requests from the redirection software made by the application programs for remote data. These requests are sent in the form of remote procedure calls (RPCs) to the communication software on the server via the communication network. The communication management software on the server makes sure that correct data is transmitted to the correct nodes.

13.1.3 Network Services Software

Network services software forms a very important module of the NOS, which is responsible for the sharable resources such as files, printers, disks, databases etc. Since there will be several clients to a single server this piece of software on the server needs to maintain a queue of the I/O requests it receives from different clients. It schedules those requests and when the turn of a specific request comes the network services software consults the information management module of the operating system running on the server to release the requested data.

Then this data traverses through the network services software and reaches the communication management software, which ensures error-free transmission via the communication network. Eventually, this data reaches the application program on the client machine traversing through the communication software, and the redirection software layers.

The main drawback of the NOS is it does not fully utilize the memory and the processing capability of all the machines on the network. Also, a user needs to be aware of different sets of commands, which are different from those he uses on his system. It will be highly advantageous if the users can access the remote resources in the same way as they access the local ones. And the distributed operating systems are designed exactly for that purpose.

13.2 Distributed Operating Systems

As said earlier, the distributed operating system has to make the best use of the resources present on the network and allocate them to various processes at a global level. The distributed operating systems possess decision-making capacity concerning the following three migrations.

13.2.1 Data Migration

Suppose that a program running on site A wants to access some data from a file residing on site B. There are two ways in which this request can be satisfied. In the first method, the entire file is transferred to site B. In this case, even if a small modification is made in the file, the entire file needs to be sent back to site A. As a result, the network gets heavily loaded. The only advantage with this approach is the less complexity involved in the design of the software to implement this scheme.

In the second method, only those portions, which the program at site B requires to carry out the execution of an immediate task, are sent. As can be guessed, this approach reduces the net traffic over the network. Also, if any portion of the file is updated only that portion is copied back to site

A. However, this scheme is very complex to implement. The network file system (NFS) of Sun Microsystems uses this approach.

13.2.2 Computation Migration

In some occasions, transferring the computation yields best results than transferring the data. For example, if a process of site A requires to produce the summary of several files residing on different machines. It will be an efficient way to access those files at their sites directly and transfer the results from there to site A instead of transferring the files directly to site A since the time to transfer the data will be more than the time to execute the remote command.

This migration of computation can be achieved in two ways: by using a remote procedure call (RPC) (we will shortly talk about this) or by sending a message to the site where from the data is to be accessed to carryout the designated task. Some intermediate processes participate in accomplishing this task.

13.2.3 Process Migration

It is the most important and equally difficult task that the distributed operating system handles. The OS has to decide which process should run on which machine and which process among several competing processes should be selected for migration. Several points need to be taken into consideration before selecting a process for migration, because of the lot of overhead involved. Some important reasons why the distributed operating systems prefer process migration are listed below:

- *Load Balancing:* With process migration it is possible to see that a specific node is completely free while another node is stuck with a heavy burden. Means, the load over the network can be made even.
- *Computation Speedup:* The system's throughput increases if a process is run as several subprocesses on different sites.

- *Special Facilities:* Some special software or hardware available at a specific node can be used by a process running on another mode.

13.3 Remote Procedure Call

The operating system contains several procedures which are responsible for such operations like locating and reading data from the disk. In order that such an operation is accomplished the procedure concerned needs to be called and if the operation is to be performed on a remote machine a *remote procedure call* should be made.

RPC can be thought of as a special case of a reliable, blocking message passing scheme. The message passed from the client containing the name of the message returned from the server contains the data resulting from the call.

A reliable service ensures that the message is received correctly by the correct node. The software module to implement this scheme consists of error correcting and error detecting codes, acknowledgement procedures etc., all of which make the software more complex. In a blocking scheme, the process on the client node gets blocked until it receives a reply from the server.

Ports: If a server node provides number of services it associates with each service a port number, which is to be specified in the network address as a part of the message sent by the RPC.

13.3.1 Calling Procedure

Similar to ordinary procedures the RPCs also allow the parameters to be passed in two methods: *call by value* and *call by reference*. In 'call by value' scheme, the actual values are passed as parameters. On the other hand, in 'call by reference' method the addresses of the actual parameters are passed to the procedure. However, in RPCs, the 'call by reference' method is not used since it is a time consuming and difficult approach to make the server node access the addresses on the client machine for the values of the parameters. The following schematic illustrates the RPC mechanism.

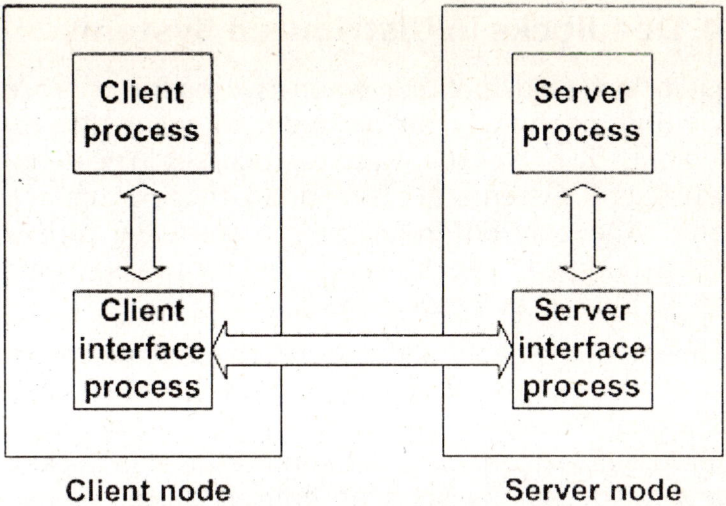

Figure 13.1 *RPC*

The interface process on both the client node and the server node handles the message at different levels. It ensures error-free communication working in accordance with different protocols at different layers. As said earlier, the RPC scheme is a blocking one. Means, the client process, upon handing over the message to the interface process, gets blocked. The interface process does the rest on behalf of the client process and ultimately gets the results. And exactly then the client process wakes up, enters the ready state and progresses with the results fetched.

The RPC scheme is heavily used in the distributed environment since it provides an easy way to implement the distributed file system about which we will be talking in the next chapter.

The speed at which a conventional RPC is executed can be enormously increased by making use of the concept of threads in RPCs. Using threads an RPC can be made more lightweight and hence a substantial gain in the speed could be achieved. There are several schemes to implement the threads package in RPCs. A comprehensive coverage of this concept is beyond the scope of this book, however.

13.4 Deadlocks in Distributed Systems

A deadlock is said to occur when two or more processes are waiting indefinitely for an event to occur that can be caused only by one of the waiting processes. The deadlocks in distributed systems are similar to those in centralized systems. The only difference lies in the ease with which they are handled. Deadlocks in distributed systems are harder to detect, avoid or prevent.

Although not very popular, there is an approved distinction between two kinds of distributed deadlocks: *resource deadlocks* and *communication deadlocks*. These terms are, of course, self-explanatory. Communication deadlocks occur on several occasions such as limited buffer space. For instance, suppose that process A wants to send some message to process B, which in turn tries to send a message to process C. Now communication deadlock occurs if the loop completes i.e., if process C also wants to send a message to process A. On the other hand, resource deadlock occurs when a fighting among several processes for a resource continues indefinitely.

In this section, we will study two famous strategies to handle deadlocks.

- Deadlock detection
- Deadlock prevention

13.4.1 Deadlock Detection

'Message passing scheme' is most commonly used to detect the occurrence of a deadlock. In this scheme, every process blocked waiting for the release of a resource forwards a special message to the current holder of that resource. For example, consider that the process P_A is waiting for a resource, which is currently held by another process, say P_B. Now, P_A sends a message to P_B. If P_B is also waiting for another resource it forwards that message to the process which held that particular resource. If the message eventually returns to P_A the deadlock is said to occur.

13.4.2 Deadlock Prevention

It proved to be a good approach to give priorities to the processes competing for the allocation of resources using the concept of aging. That means a process that waits longer will have a higher priority. Now, these ranked processes are dealt to resolve the conflict. There are two widely followed schemes:

- Wait-die technique
- Wound-wait technique

Wait-die

This is a non-preemptive scheme in which the process requesting a resource is permitted to wait if it is older than the process currently holding the resource. Otherwise, the requesting process is killed and made start all over again.

Wound-wait

This is a pre-emptive scheme. In this technique, the requesting process waits for the release of the resource if it is younger than the process currently holding the resource. Otherwise, it kills that process and gains access to that resource.

13.5 Failure Detection, Reconfiguration and Recovery

A distributed system, which is built using unreliable communication links, always suffers from various types of hardware failure. A system can be declared robust when proper measures are taken to detect such failures. The system is reconfigured and recovered when the link is repaired.

13.5.1 Failure Detection

There are several types of failures in a distributed system like link failure, site failure and message loss. However, it is not precisely possible to find out which type of failure has occurred. For example, consider two sites A and B. Suppose that we want to detect whether there is any failure between the sites A and B, the site A being the point to conduct the test. Then we send a message from site A to B, setting a time slice.

In the absence of any failure, the acknowledgement for the message should reach site A before the time slice expires. If the reply doesn't arrive in proper time, it can be concluded that there is a failure between the sites A and B. To detect whether the failure is in the physical link, the message can be resent via an alternate link. If the site B responds to this message properly it can be decided that the problem is with the link.

13.5.2 Reconfiguration

If it is detected that a site in the network is failed, each site in the system must be notified about it so that they can alter their routing tables and stop using the resources of that site. The site which detects a failure should initiate a procedure which allows the system to reconfigure it.

13.5.3 Recovery From Failure

When the attempts to repair a site result in a success that site needs to be rejoined in the system. This site should notify all other sites in the system of its resources so that they can alter their tables and consider the resources of this site for their use.

13.6 Design Issues

In this section, we will study some basic issues that help the designers bring out the future distributed systems, which can cope up with the ever increasing demands despite certain technological limitations.

13.6.1 New Hardware

As we know, the main purpose of any software is to provide

such an environment to the user where he can execute his programs conveniently and efficiently. The software makes the operation of hardware easy for the user. The complexity of the software varies with the complexity of the hardware with which it has to deal. Sometimes a small modification in the hardware (like adding a chip) might reduce the difficulty in coding the software to a greater extent. Hence, the researchers should concentrate on bringing out new hardware that can simplify the job of software designers.

13.6.2 Scalability

The latest trend in distributed systems is towards larger systems. A system is called scalable if it adapts itself to the increasing service load without subjecting any user to despair. But the resources a system possesses are limited and eventually they would fail to meet the demand of the increasing load. Although adding new resources appears to be a remedy it causes another problem of increasing the service load. The network may fail to handle the increased traffic. Hence, care should be taken in designing the system itself so that the system can withstand high service load and allow new users also to make use of its services.

13.6.3 Mobility

In a transparent system, the user will be able to access all the resources in the entire system as his local ones. A transparent distributed system should support mobility. That means the user should not be restricted to work only on a specific machine. His working environment should be brought to whatever system he logs into.

13.6.4 Fault Tolerance

Most of the computer systems today are not fault tolerant. A fault-tolerant system should function without break despite failures and degradations. However, it is not practically possible to implement a fault-tolerant system. However, with the help of specific amount of redundancy in hardware and also in software some fault tolerance can be achieved.

Review Questions

1. What is a network operating system?
2. What are the different software modules of network operating system?
3. What is the significance of redirection software in a network operating system?
4. What is a distributed operating system?
5. Explain process migration.
6. Explain the concept of RPC in detail.
7. What is a port?
8. Explain the most widely used calling procedure in the RPC scheme.
9. In what way deadlocks in distributed systems differ from their counterparts in centralized systems?
10. Explain the key issues to be studied while designing a distributed system.

CHAPTER

14

Distributed File Management

Introduction

This chapter discusses in detail the distributed file system. It describes the cache management in distributed processing. The necessity of file replication in a distributed environment is explained. The security measures required are also discussed.

14.1 Distributed File System

In the NOS environment, the user needs to specify the location of the file explicitly before he makes a request to access it. Such a specification is not necessary in the distributed environment because the user can access a file as if it were present in his local file system.

As we have studied in a chapter on centralized file management, there can be several operations performed on a file or directory. They include reading from a file, writing in a file, appending to a file, truncating a file etc. In a distributed environment, the user will be able to perform all these operations on any file or directory even though it is not a part of his local file system. The distributed file system allows him to do so. This illustration can be visualized by observing the following example.

Consider four users A, B, C and D in a distributed environment. Each user has his own local file system on his disk as illustrated in figure 14.1.

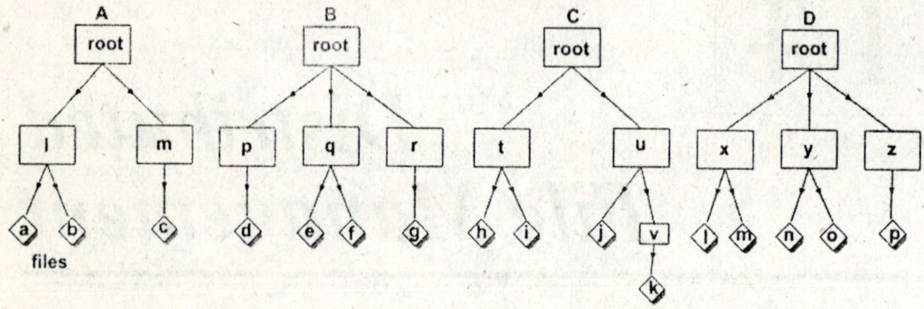

Figure 14.1 *Different local file systems*

Each user wants to view the file systems of other users in his file system. For instance, the user A may want to see as if the file systems of users B, C and D were under his root directory. Then the virtual file system under the root directory of A will be as illustrated in figure 14.2.

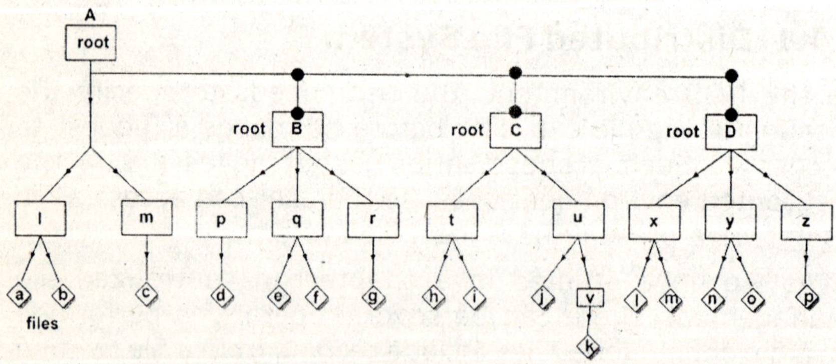

Figure 14.2 *Virtual file system as seen by A*

Implementing such a virtual file system is not an easy task. For instance, each of the other 3 users might also want to have their own virtual systems. And, more significantly, *the views of the users will differ*. As can be guessed, catering to the diverging ideas of all these four users simultaneously is not an ordinary task. If that much complexity is involved in realizing the dream of virtual file system in the case of just four users, one can easily guess how laborious the task would be to manage thousands and thousands of users separated by hundreds of miles in a distributed environment.

14.2 Naming

A constructive research in the area of naming the files in the distributed file system hinted at the possibility of realizing the dream of achieving a virtual file system that caters to the needs and perceptions of all the users in the system.

The users make use of file names to deal with logical data and the system deals with physical blocks of data, stored in disk sectors. 'Naming' is the necessary mapping between logical and physical objects. This mapping occurs at a number of levels whose ultimate aim is to hide such details like how and where the file is actually stored on the disk. Similarly, in a DFS it is to be hidden from the user where in the network the file is located to make the file system a transparent one.

There are two distinct notions in this regard:

14.2.1 Location Independence

In this scheme, the path name of the file doesn't have to change when the file is transferred from one location to another. The backbone to this scheme is the idea to replicate the files. File replication is the concept in which multiple copies of the same file appear on different nodes. The DFS maintains a table that consists of the details of each file and the nodes where the file is kept. When a request is made for a file this table is referred to and taking into account the transmission time from each node containing that file, the location to transfer the file from is chosen and then the mapping from logical name to the physical location is done dynamically.

14.2.2 Location Transparency

In this scheme, a user needs to define his perception of the virtual composite directory structure. Means, he needs to decide in advance which files or directories should reside on which nodes. The DFS provides several protocols and commands for the user to define his own view of the composite file system. Location transparency provides the users with a convenient environment to share the commands. The user in a location transparent distributed system can access a file by simply using its name as if it were present on his local file system.

14.3 Cache Management

The traffic in the network heavily affects the performance of a system. Hence, the main goal of any intelligent design would be to reduce the network traffic making use of the strength of certain advantageous concepts like 'caching'.

14.3.1 Cache Location

In one of the previous chapters we have studied the 'track-at-a-time' caching scheme in which an entire track is cached while serving the request for a single sector on that track. This scheme is taken further in a distributed environment. Multiple buffers are provided at different locations in the network which serve as cache locations.

In a client-server environment, there can be four locations where the desired data can reside. They are:

- The client station's buffer
- The client station's disk
- The server's buffer
- The server's disk

It is obvious that a user's request is satisfied at a faster rate if the desired blocks of data are found in the local buffer itself. On the other extreme, if the data requested resides on the server's disk it will take a longer time to access that data. Also the network traffic poses a problem.

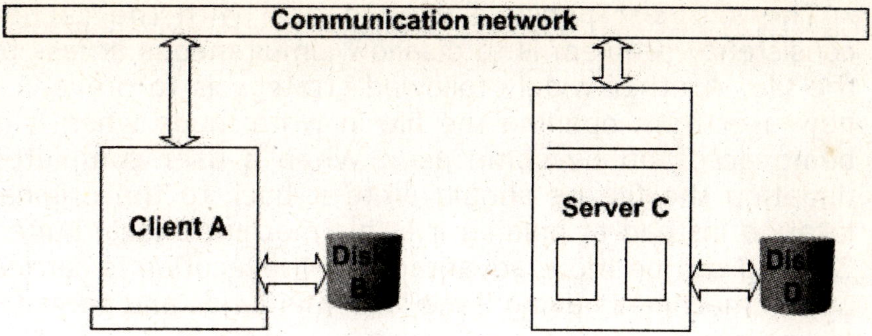

Figure 14.3 *Cache management*

In figure 14.3, A, B, C and D represent the client's buffer, client's disk, server's buffer and server's disk respectively. The best desired location for the data to reside is A, and the least desired one is D. These two form the extremities. The main objective of cache management scheme is to keep the most heavily referenced blocks at location A so that the future requests for referencing those blocks can be satisfied at a faster rate. The cache management uses algorithms like 'most recently used algorithm' to decide which blocks to keep at location A. However, the location A might get completely occupied by data and there might be no room for holding the newly cached blocks. When this situation arises some blocks need to be overwritten by the newly arriving blocks. These blocks to overwrite are selected using the 'least recently used' algorithm.

14.3.2 Cache Consistency

The cache management makes the user work with the copy of the original file which resides on the server's disk. The original file is called master copy. Several copies of the original file will be on a number of client machines. The user, after making manipulations in the copy version, replaces the master copy with it. Now, imagine what happens if several users using the same file update it simultaneously? Which one should be saved? Undoubtedly, some will be lost if simultaneous updates are made. This problem is referred to as 'cache consistency'. If the users open the file in 'read-only' mode, nothing untowardly happens. The problem arises only when the file is opened in 'read-write' mode.

The simplest possible way to deal with the cache-consistency problem is to disallow simultaneous access to the file. Another widely followed strategy is to prevent a new user from opening the file in write mode when it is being accessed by some user. When a user completes updating the file he should write it back to the original location instead of holding it in his machine's local buffer. Caching can be more advantageous if execution is carried out on machines having large local memories and personal disks.

14.4 Security

As is the case with computer science always, we do not get something for nothing. So far, we have discussed with amazement the various services that a user in a distributed environment can enjoy. We talked at length about different topologies and switching strategies. We wondered at the power of scalable and fault-tolerant systems. We dreamed about the 'virtual file system'. Altogether, we approved the concept of distributed systems with a lot of enthusiasm. However, there is an important corner to through some light on. We need to talk about the disastrous effects that an insecure system may be subjected to.

14.4.1 Overview

Security is a very important issue which is given paramount importance by researchers and system designers. An entire chapter has been devoted to discuss about various security threats and appropriate remedies in this book. In this section, we will have a very brief look at security in a distributed environment.

A system is said to be insecure if any person is able to access the resources, for instance data, without proper authentication. In a non-distributed system the measures taken by the operating system to counter act the security threats are sufficient. However, in a distributed system there will be gigabytes of information and also the number of malicious attempts will be significantly higher. For instance, denying access to vital information such as central password table might serve the purpose in a non-networked single system. But the scenario in the case of systems that make use of network services is widely different.

For example, consider that a message passes from node A to X via a number of intermediate nodes. What happens if one of these intermediate nodes is captured by an unauthentic user? Certainly, he will be able to modify the contents of that message. To combat this all the links in the network need to be properly guarded. This approach is termed as 'link oriented measure'. However, such an approach tends to be expensive because the cost to ensure secure and safe passage of message from one node to another depends upon the number of intermediate nodes. Hence, another scheme known as 'end-to-end' approach is followed in which only the end systems pay for the security cost. That means, in the above example, the nodes A and X only pay for the security service they require.

14.4.2 Encryption

Encrypting the message using certain encryption algorithms and passing them to the destination node along with a specific key has been another interesting way to deal with the problem of security threats. The destination node uses the appropriate decryption algorithms to decipher the message. The utilization of a key prevents any Intruder from attempting to decode the message. These keys are of two types: public key and private key. The private key is known to only two processes: the process sending the encrypted message and the process receiving the message. The public key can be made known to every one using which any process can communicate with the process sending the encrypted message.

14.5 NFS

In this section, we will briefly study the network file system (NFS) introduced by Sun Microsystems in 1984. NFS uses the Unreliable Datagram Protocol/Internet Protocol (UDP/IP) on top of Ethernet as a communication protocol. With NFS one can easily access remote files without modifying or relinking any program.

NFS preserved UNIX semantics. Hence, the notions of file access permissions and privileges resemble those of UNIX versions. However, NFS can easily be ported to different operating systems running on various machines.

Figure 14.4 illustrates NFS functionality. It shows both client node and server node and various components of each node.

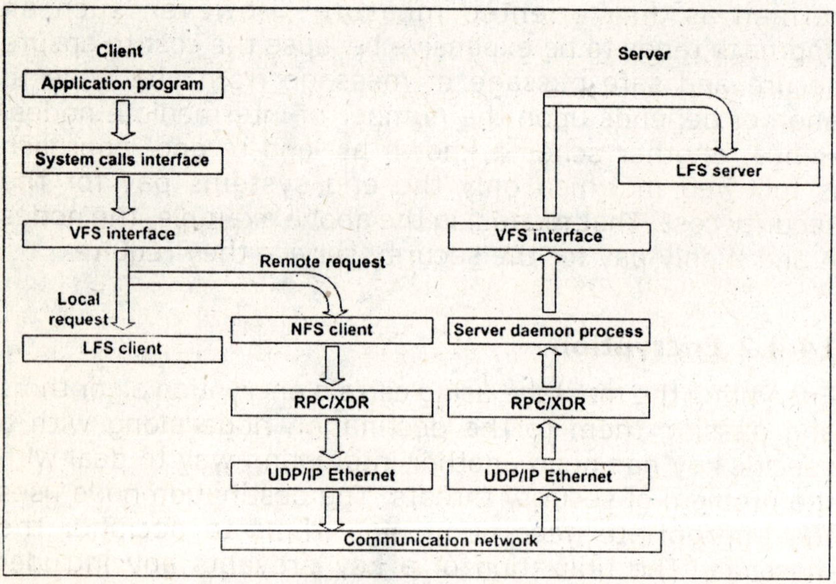

Figure 14.4 *NFS architecture*

In the figure, VFS stands for virtual file system about which we have discussed previously.

The initial logical connection between the client and server is established with the help of the *mount* protocol. This protocol is responsible for two actions: exporting and mounting. By means of the exporting mechanism all the nodes in the system become aware of all the sharable file systems. Mounting is a process by which a user selects the file systems from the pool of available ones.

'Daemons' are the NFS interface processes, which are initiated by NFS after the system is booted. They are responsible for getting and servicing the remote requests coming from the clients. RPC/XDR is a software layer. We have discussed about RPC in the previous chapter. XDR is similar to the presentation layer. This is provided to deal with different types of machines.

Let us now trace the steps that are followed when a client accesses a remote file.

- An application program running on the client's machine makes a request for some data.
- The system-calls interface translates this request into a system call and passes it to the VFS interface.
- At the VFS interface it is checked whether the request is for local or remote data. If it is for local data the request is passed to the LFS. Otherwise, it is translated into appropriate NFS calls. These calls are initiated on the client machine one by one and the server machine processes each NFS call separately. After a call is processed the control is passed to the client and then the clients VFS interface initiates another call. Eventually, the request is completely satisfied.

Thus, this chapter presented a brief study about distributed file management, one of the challenging topics.

Review Questions

1. What is a virtual file system?
2. What is the main difficulty in designing a VFS?
3. What are the different naming strategies?
4. What are the various cache locations in a distributed system?
5. Explain the cache consistency problem.
6. Why providing security is more important in a distributed system?
7. How encrypting the message to be sent results advantageous in a distributed system?
8. Explain NFS in detail.

CHAPTER

15

UNIX: A Case Study

Introduction

This chapter is a case study in UNIX, a multiuser, multitasking operating system developed by Ken Thompson and Dennis Ritchie in Bell Labs. The first version of UNIX came out in 1969.

Any operating system offers its services through two interfaces: user interface and system call interface. There are two separable parts in UNIX: the kernel and the systems programs. The kernel plays a very important role by providing the mechanisms to manage the file system and memory through system calls. The systems programs make use of these system calls to provide several useful functions to the users. In UNIX, the system calls define the *programmer interface* and the set of systems programs define the *user interface*.

15.1 Programmer Interface

There are three categories into which the system calls in UNIX can be divided:

- File manipulation

- Process control
- Information manipulation

15.1.1 File Manipulation

In UNIX, a file is a sequence of bytes. The files are organized in directories, which are also files treated in a different manner.

For basic file manipulation there are some system calls in UNIX like *creat*, *open*, *close*, *read*, *write*, *trunc* etc. The *creat* system call creates a new file, given a path name. The *open* system call opens an existing file, which requires the path name and the mode of operation (read, write etc.) as parameters, and returns an integer known as *file descriptor*. This file descriptor may then be passed to *read* or *write* system calls to read from or write to a file. The *trunc* call is used to reduce the length of the file to 0.

The commonly used system calls for directory manipulation are *mkdir*, *cd*, *rmdir* etc. The system call *mkdir* is used to make a new directory. Similarly, *cd* is used to change the presently working directory and *rmdir* is used to remove (delete) a directory.

15.1.2 Process Control

As we have studied in one of the previous chapters, a process can be treated as a program under execution. The system call *fork* is used to create a new process. The system call *execve* is used after the *fork* system call to load a binary file into active memory and execute it. A process uses the *exit* system call to terminate. If a process is exiting, its parent process may wait to know which of its many child processes is exiting using the *wait* system call.

15.1.3 Information Manipulation

There exist system calls to set and return an interval timer (*get timer/set timer*) and to set and return the current time (*get time of day/set time of day*).

15.2 User Interface

As is said earlier, the set of systems programs defines the user interface in UNIX. The systems programs are readily executable programs, which make the necessary system calls to support their function.

These systems programs and the user programs are executed by a command interpreter, which is known as shell in UNIX. There are several shells developed like Bourne shell, C shell etc. UNIX is normally an interactive operating system. That means, the user types a command at the command prompt and presses the Enter key to observe the output of that command. Consider the following example:

$ ls

In the above statement '$' is known as the shell prompt and *ls* is the command whose purpose is to list the files in the presently working directory. Once the user presses the Enter key after typing *ls* at the prompt, all the files and directories in the presently working directory are listed.

The output of one process can be redirected as the input to another process using pipes. Pipes function very effectively as the means of communication between the processes. A pipe is a queue of bytes between two processes that can be accessed as an ordinary file through a file descriptor. If one process writes to one end of the pipe, the other process reads from the other end. This pipe lining may be extended to any number of processes. A vertical bar '|' is used to represent the pipe in UNIX.

15.3 UNIX File System

The file system of UNIX is hierarchical in nature, which starts with a root directory at the top level. The root directory contains several directories and files. These directories in turn contain several other subdirectories and files and this hierarchical structure continues like that. Figure 15.1 gives the diagrammatical representation of the UNIX file system in which diamonds represent files and squares represent directories.

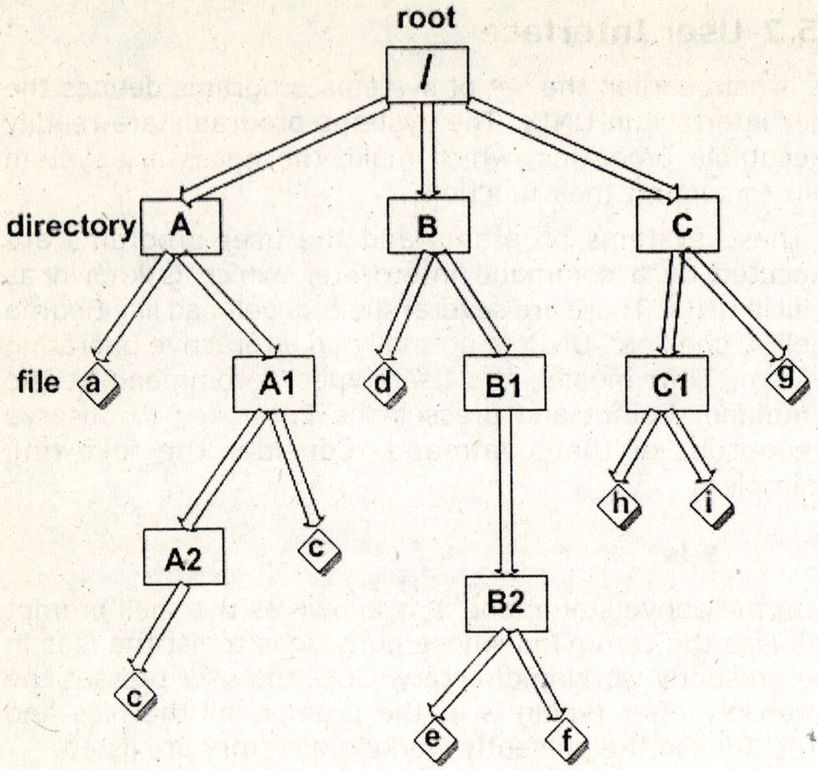

Figure 15.1 *UNIX file system*

Files and directories are the two main objects supported by the UNIX file system. Directories are also files but with a special format. They contain number of records or entries, each entry corresponding to a file or subdirectory under that directory.

An *inode* (index node) represents a file on the disk. The inode is a record that maintains the information about the file or directory such as its owner, access rights, last modification date and pointers to various disk blocks allocated to it etc. The 'type' field in the inode (pointer) distinguishes a directory from a file.

15.3.1 Mounting / Unmounting Files in UNIX

It is a good idea to partition a single disk to house several file-systems, each file system starting with its own root directory. Multiple file systems result if a system has multiple disks attached to it. Now, it is an interesting task to copy a file from one file system to another. Let us consider two disks C and D having the file structures as shown in the figure 15.2.

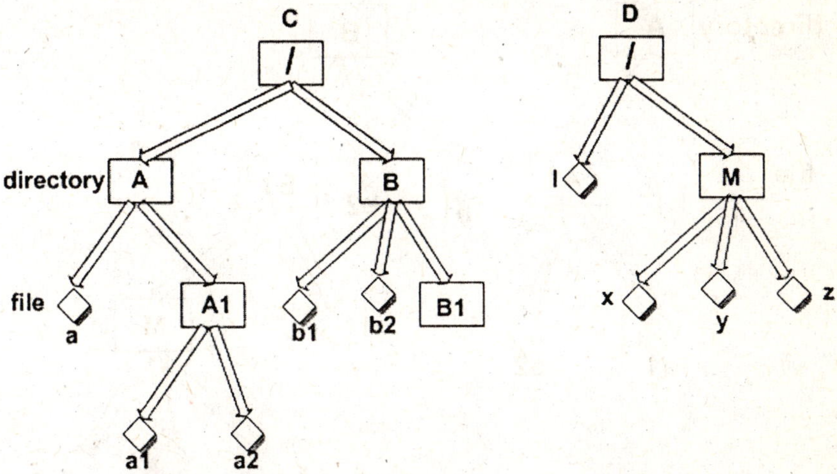

Figure 15.2 *Drives C and D before mounting*

Now let us consider that we want to copy the file y in the directory M of drive D into the directory B of drive C. Using the following DOS command it may be accomplished.

cp D:\M\y C:\B\y

But the strategy followed by UNIX in this case is different. It follows the entire directory structure of D to be mounted on drive C under a specific directory, say B1 of drive C. This can be accomplished by a simple *mount* command. The file structure appears as shown below after mounting:

Now the file *y* can simply be copied to the directory A with a simple command

cp /B/B1/M/y /A/A1/y

Similar to this mounting, unmounting a file system can also be done to separate it from another file system with a separate root directory. It is a facility offered to the user by

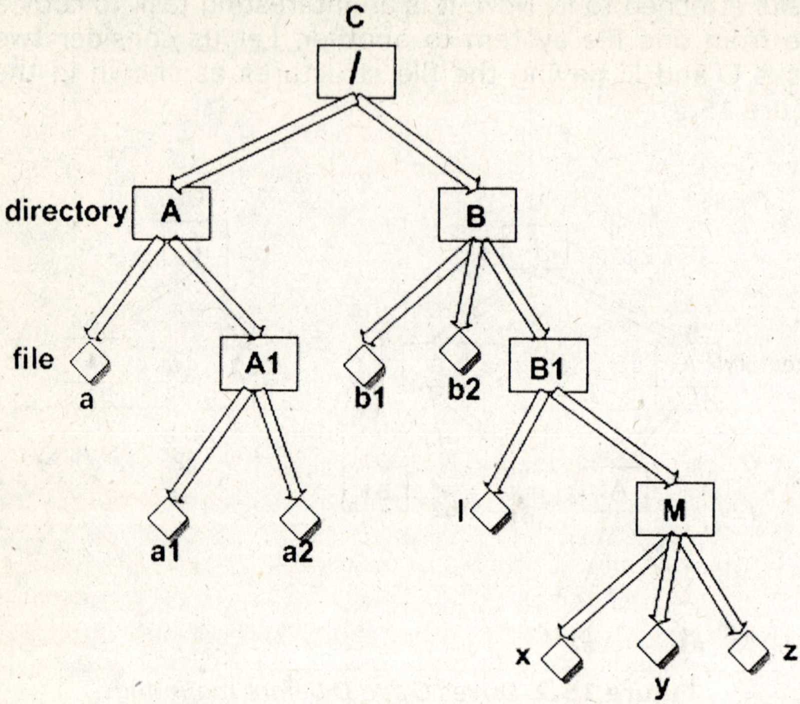

Figure 15.3 *Drive C after mounting drive D*

UNIX to mount or unmount a file system at a pre-specified time. With mounting and unmounting the security of the system can be enhanced further.

15.3.2 The Internals of UNIX File System

The file system in UNIX can be considered to be divided into four different logical parts as shown in figure 15.4.

The first block is known as 'boot block' because it contains the boot or boot strap program. Immediately after the system is switched ON the hardware reads from this block.

The second block is known as 'super block', which contains the information about the file system. The super block is normally more than one block in length.

The blocks III and IV constitute the allocable blocks. Block III is reserved for inodes and block IV consists of data blocks that can be allocated to different files.

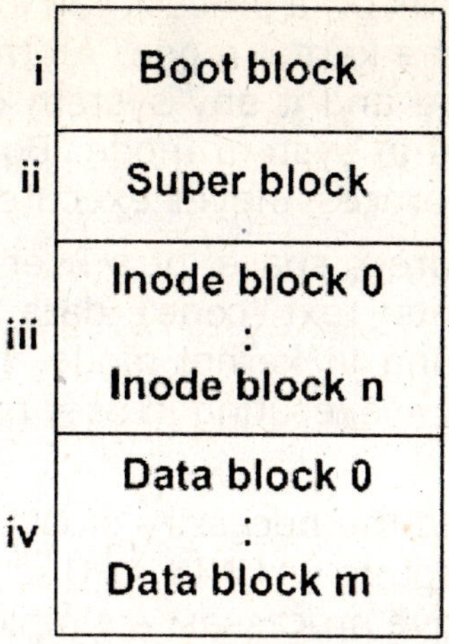

Figure 15.4 *UNIX file system internals*

The super block maintains a *partial* list of free blocks, which is known as 'super block cache' (There will be further more blocks outside the super block to hold the numbers of the free blocks). Whenever a request for a free block is made, the system refers to the super block cache and allocates that free block. The last entry in the super block represents the number of the free block that holds the number of next (specific number of) free blocks. When all the free blocks pointed by the super block cache are allocated, it is refreshed with new entries and the same process repeats.

15.4 Process Management

As we have seen already - a process is a program under execution. UNIX provides a facility to create a new process even when there is no sufficient memory to accommodate it. This newly created process is entered the *ready but swapped* state if there is not enough memory. If the free memory available is sufficient to accommodate a newly created process, it directly enters the *ready* state.

The processes in UNIX are represented by various control blocks. The information held by these control blocks is used by the kernel for carrying out certain operations like CPU scheduling etc. In UNIX, a process can execute either in the user mode or in the kernel mode. All the ordinary work is done in user mode and if any system calls are made the work is performed in system mode. Both the system and user phases of a process never execute simultaneously.

The 'virtual address space' of a user process is divided into three segments: text (code), data and stack. When a process is executing in kernel mode, the kernel stack is used. And when it is executing in user mode the user stack is used.

We have studied the necessity of CPU scheduling in one of the previous chapters. In UNIX, CPU scheduling is designed to benefit interactive processes. A simple priority algorithm is used as the scheduling algorithm, which reduces to a Round Robin algorithm for CPU bound processes. The technique of aging is used to prevent starvation.

A scheduling priority will be attached to every process, which is used in determining when the CPU could be allocated to it. The smaller the number is, the higher the priority will be.

In kernel, no process can preempt another. A process executing in kernel relinquishes the CPU only when it decides to sleep on an event i.e., when it is waiting on I/O, for example. Of course, it needs to relinquish the CPU if the time slice for which the CPU is allocated to it expires.

15.5 Memory Management

In the earlier chapters, we have considered the basic principles of memory management. Also, we have discussed several memory management schemes. In UNIX, swapping and demand paging are the 2 most extensively used memory management schemes. We will consider them here again in brief.

15.5.1 Swapping

Swapping is used when keeping the entire process image in main memory becomes a requirement. If a process with a higher priority arrives when there is not sufficient memory to accommodate it, a process with a lower priority is swapped out on to a 'swapping device'. When the turn of this 'swapped out' process comes it is 'swapped in' to the physical memory. Only the kernel can read data from or write the data to the swap device. The allocation is done contiguously in the case of swap device to achieve higher speeds.

15.5.2 Demand Paging

The important points to be noted here are:

- The process image is divided into equal sized pages and the physical memory is divided into same sized frames. (That means, one page size = one frame size).
- When a process needs to be brought into physical memory, depending upon the space available, some frames are allocated to it, which might be less than required. So, eventually page fault occurs and then that required page is loaded. As this process continues it may happen that the available physical memory is not sufficient to load a demanded page. Then an old page is replaced by the demanded page. The page replacement algorithm decides which page is to be replaced. In UNIX, LRU (least recently used) algorithm is used.
- If the page to be replaced is modified and needs to be saved before getting swapped out, the kernel writes the same onto the swap file so that it can locate it and load it back next time.

15.6 I/O System

It is one of the duties of the operating system to hide the peculiarities of certain hardware devices from the user. The I/O system maintains a buffer caching system, drivers and general device driver code for certain hardware it supports. Only the corresponding driver of a hardware device knows its peculiarities.

Block devices, character devices and socket interface

are the three major kinds of I/O supported by the latest versions of UNIX.

Block devices include tapes and disks, where as terminals, line printers and almost everything else that do not use block-buffering cache come under the category of character devices. The character devices receive/transmit data one character at a time and the block devices receive/transmit one block at a time.

There will be two arrays of entry points to access the device drivers. One array is for character devices and the other is for block devices. The *device number* and the *class* are used to distinguish one device from another. The device type is called the *major number* and the device number within that type is called the *minor number*. If we want to write a character to a terminal, we need to execute the device driver for terminals using the major number and then pass the minor number, which is specific terminal id, as a parameter. If there exist two different terminals they will have two major numbers because they will be treated as two different types requiring different device drivers.

15.7 Booting and Login

In this section, we will study what happens immediately after the system is switched on to work with UNIX.

15.7.1 Booting

The process of loading the UNIX kernel system into memory, executing it and thus making the system ready for the users is known as booting.

The 'bootable disk' contains the 'boot program' in its booting block. The booting block is generally the first block in the file system. This program is executed immediately when the system is switched ON.

15.7.2 Login Process

- For the user to login the init process creates the child process *getty* for every active communication line i.e., if there are 10 terminals, init creates *getty* for each one.

- *getty* waits for the user to type in an input, which is his/her login name. As soon as the user types in a character *getty* picks it up and stores it.
- After the user completes typing the login name and presses the Enter key, *getty* passes this login name to another process '*login*', which it spawns as its child process, as an argument.
- The login process then accesses the file */etc/passwd*, which contains the login names and passwords of all the users, and checks for the validity of this login name.
- If the name entered is valid, the *login* process prompts for the password and accepts the password keyed in by the user.
- This password is then compared with that stored in / *etc/passwd* in encrypted form, for that user.
- If both of them do not match an error message id displayed and the user is given another chance to make an attempt again.
- After three consecutive unsuccessful attempts the *login* process prints on the screen another error message and terminates.
- Then, the *login* process checks for new messages and mails in the corresponding files for this user and if there are any, it displays them.
- Now, as the last part of the login procedure, the shell process is spawned by the *execve* system call.
- Now, the shell runs the appropriate system login scripts to initialize the user environment. Then the shell runs the users' local login script, if it exists in the home directory of that user.

Thus the shell is ready to accept the commands from the user.

Figure 15.5 gives the sequentlal representation of the login process hierarchies.

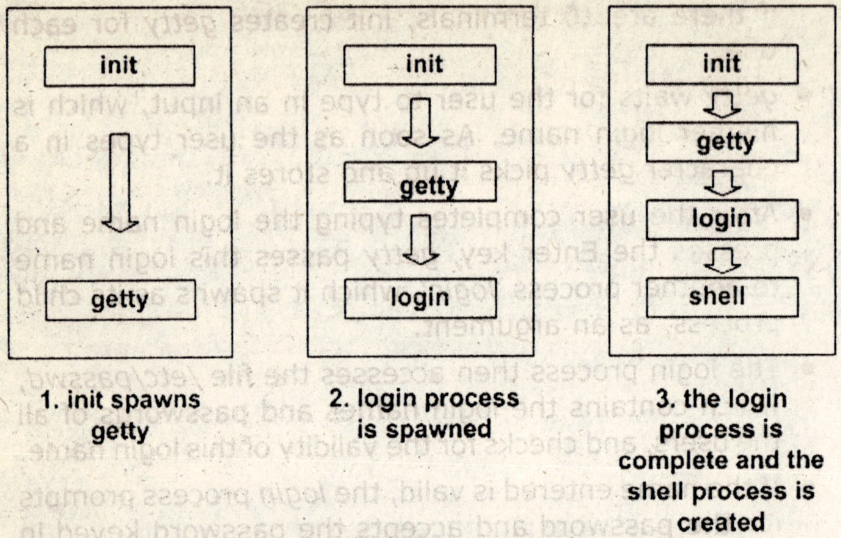

Figure 15.5 *Login process*

Thus, this is a brief case study in UNIX.

Review Questions

1. What are the different interfaces in UNIX?
2. Explain the programmer interface in UNIX.
3. Explain the UNIX file system.
4. Explain process management in UNIX.
5. Explain how the memory is managed in UNIX.
6. Explain, in detail, the login process in UNIX.

Index

N

O

P

R

S